THE
MUM'S
POCKET BIBLE

THE
MUM'S
POCKET BIBLE

HANNAH DORAN

This edition first published in Great Britain 2010 by
Crimson Publishing, a division of Crimson Business Ltd
Westminster House
Kew Road
Richmond
Surrey
TW9 2ND

A catalogue record for this book is available from the British Library.

ISBN 978 1 907087 01 1

Printed and bound by L.E.G.O. SpA, Trento.

For Ines, Edith and Danny

ACKNOWLEDGEMENTS

I would like to thank my mother, Liz Doran, and my mother-in-law, Jenny Hancock, for their sterling examples of patient and practical motherhood and, of course, their wonderful childcare, without which I could not have completed this book.

Thanks also to the lovely mothers of SW15 for their support–in particular, to Heidi Stevens and Suya Skanthan for the tea and cake. Special thanks to Robyn Harper for her bobotie recipe, Jamie Hussey for the wart remedy, and Kate Leigh-Wood for the sloe gin recipe.

Thanks also to the Crimson Publishing team: Sally Rawlings, Beth Bishop and Holly Ivins.

Finally I have to thank Ines, Edith and Danny, who have been the patient guinea-pigs for recipes and activities throughout the writing of this book. And Tom, for his enthusiasm and support, for which I don't thank him enough.

CONTENTS

INTRODUCTION

Whatever else is unsure in this stinking dunghill of a world,
a mother's love is not.
James Joyce

Defining the characterishics of a mother is infinitely complex: what was once the straightforward role of nurturer has been amplified and expanded, with a greater and welcome focus on the mother as a person in her own right. Mothers are now routinely expected to be all things to all people: cook, cleaner, plumber, teacher, taxi-driver, seamstress, gardener, accountant and nurse. The modern mum sustains her own career and contributes to the family funds while also maintaining her responsibilities as a part-ner and lover, and a role model for her children. Add to that the demands of ensuring a healthy and green lifestyle for the whole family. Oh, and it's meant to be fun. No wonder we're exhausted! Caring for children can be the most rewarding and least satisfying job in the world – usually at the same time.

Therefore, this book doesn't attempt to label mothers with easy tags such as 'alpha', 'yummy' or, God forbid, 'slummy'. Rather, it is intended as a practical reference guide to help with the many chores, duties, undertakings and roles that motherhood often encompasses. It is squarely aimed at making day-to-day life that bit easier.

Pocket fact 🌱

'Mother' was voted as the favourite English word in a survey by the British Council in 2004.

Whether you have to organise a fifth birthday party, rustle up Sunday lunch for two families, interview a childminder, or help your teenager with a university application, this book will give you top tips and the tools for the task at hand. Furthermore, it is a celebration of the dexterous nature of all mothers, young and old: that incredible capacity (and dare I say, essentially *female* ability) to perform all of the above tasks *at the same time*.

❁ MOTHER'S DAY ❁

Contrary to popular belief, Mother's Day was not dreamt up by card manufacturers. The earliest celebration of motherhood can be traced to the annual spring festival of the ancient Greeks, dedicated to the goddess Rhea, and to the Roman festival of Matronalia, which celebrated Juno.

In England the tradition began in the 16th century for people to return to their 'mother' church or cathedral once a year, usually during Lent; this was referred to as going 'a mothering'. It was also an opportunity for families, geographically separated through work, to reunite, and hence the occasion evolved into a celebration of mothers. Servant girls were given the day off on the fourth Sunday in Lent to visit their families. Picking a posy of flowers as they walked home or carrying a Simnel cake began the tradition of giving your mother a small gift to mark the occasion.

> *I'll to thee a Simnell bring,*
> *'Gainst thou go'st a mothering,*
> *So that, when she blesseth thee,*
> *Half that blessing thou'lt give to me.*
> Robert Herrick, 1648

Nowadays, Mother's Day is the biggest card-sending celebration after Christmas and Valentine's Day. Despite the inevitable commercial spin, there remains something welcoming about thismore formal opportunity to recognise and give thanks to our mothers.

Happy Mother's Day, every day.

FEEDING THE TROOPS: MEALS FOR YOUR FAMILY

❀ WEEKLY MEAL PLANNING ❀

There is nothing more guaranteed to take the fun out of cooking than the daily demands of providing food day after day for a hungry family. Not to mention the hours wasted wandering blankly round a supermarket trying to think of something healthy and interesting to do with lamb chops.

Meal planning sounds like yet another chore but it saves time and money as well as ensuring that your family eats a variety of foods. Here's how to come up with a meal plan with minimum fuss:

1. First, check your store cupboards and freezer and aim to use what is already there.

2. Write a list of at least 15 meals that your family enjoys.

3. Now plan your week, choosing each dinner and lunch, and making allowances for days when you are particularly busy or won't feel like cooking.

4. Plan to cook double quantities on some nights to freeze or use later in the week, or batch-cook all-purpose foods, such as tomato sauce and bolognese, which can be frozen and used at short notice.

5. Think about what meals are suitable for all the family to cut down on the cooking – roast dinners for example need not be restricted to Sundays and usually appeal to children and adults alike.

6. Once the menu is written, write your shopping list, remembering to add staples such as cereals and bread.

7. Shake things up by trying a new recipe every Monday or eat vegetarian twice a week.

8. Get the children involved in deciding the menu: they are more likely to eat dinner if they helped to choose it.

Pocket tip 🦋

Shopping online saves time and removes the temptation to overspend. All the main supermarkets now offer home delivery — but compare charges and make sure you get the best deal for you. They also offer different time slots, from one to three hours. You might not want to be stuck at home waiting for the doorbell to ring for three hours, so pick accordingly.

STORE CUPBOARD ESSENTIALS

Keep your kitchen cupboards well-stocked and you will have the means to create a delicious meal even when the fridge is bare.

- **Dried pasta**. Keep a variety to maximise its use: twisted pasta (fusilli, fettuccine, farfalle) is best for thin, oily sauces such as pesto; tubular pasta (rigatoni, penne, macaroni) for baked dishes, and long thin pasta (spaghetti, linguine) for bolognese and tomato sauces.

- **Tinned tomatoes**. The essential ingredient for many soups, stews, sauces and curries. For a simple pasta dish, simmer one 400g tin slowly with one chopped onion and two sliced garlic cloves for 20 minutes, stir in mascarpone, and serve with spaghetti and freshly grated Parmesan.

- **Rice**. Serve as an accompaniment to curries, chilli and stews, or use Arborio rice for a main course risotto.

- **Couscous**. A quicker alternative to rice and pasta. Add peas or chopped dried apricots for extra flavour.

- **Bouillon**. Create instant stock or use to add flavour to couscous, soups and risotto.

- **Pesto**. Not just for pasta: spread on chicken or white fish and grill for a quick supper.

- **Olive oil**. A healthier alternative to butter for frying: use extra virgin for salad dressings or to dress steamed vegetables.

- **Vinegar**. Keep a variety of vinegars for marinades, salad dressings, and stir fries.

FRIDGE ESSENTIALS

- **Cheese**. Keep cheddar and Parmesan in stock to add to pasta, risotto, make toasties, rarebit and the essential cheese sandwich. Wrap in plastic and keep in the salad drawer.

- **Lemons**. Will keep in the fridge for up to two weeks and can be used to add much needed flavour and zest to all sorts of dishes. Combine freshly cooked spaghetti with the juice and fine zest of two lemons, two large handfuls of grated Parmesan, one handful of torn fresh basil and 200ml of good olive oil for a fresh and light supper dish.

- **Milk**. Children under five should be given whole milk. Blend with a banana and a handful of strawberries for a yummy and healthy milkshake. Sour milk can be used to make scones.

- **Eggs**. Scramble, poach, boil or fry. Butter a ramekin and layer sliced ham, spinach and a dash of ketchup, topped by an egg and grated cheese. Bake in the oven for coddled eggs: the perfect quick supper.

- **Butter**. Keep both salted and unsalted (for baking). Buy in bulk and store extra in the freezer to avoid running out.

- **Crème fraiche/mascarpone**. Heat gently and add grated cheddar for a quick cheese sauce; blend with fruits and chill to make fool; or use instead of cream to fill a sponge cake.

- **Bacon**. Adds bags of flavour to a variety of stews, pasta dishes, quiches or the good old English breakfast.

FREEZER ESSENTIALS

The freezer is an invaluable aid to the mother faced with an empty cupboard and hungry children. Keep your freezer stocked with these basics and you will always have a meal on hand.

- **Green vegetables**. As nutritious as fresh vegetables, the most useful and child-friendly varieties are peas, green beans, sweet-corn and spinach.

- **Root vegetables**. When chopping root vegetables, double the quantities and freeze in sandwich bags to use in soups, roast from frozen, or add to stews. A combination of sweet potato, swede, butternut squash and carrot works well.

- **Summer fruits**. Heat gently from frozen with a table spoon of sugar for an easy dessert.

- **Fish fillets**. Oven-bake, grill or poach from frozen.

- **Stock**. Freeze stock and/or leftover wine in ice cube trays, then decant into freezer bags to use as and when needed.

- **Breadcrumbs**. Make in large quantities and freeze in small amounts. Combine with egg and use to coat chicken or fish to make nuggets. Add lemon, onion and Dijon mustard to make an instant stuffing for oily fish or roast chicken.

- **Pitta bread**. Pop in the toaster straight from the freezer and fill with tuna or grated cheese and cucumber.

- **Shortcrust pastry**. Choose ready-rolled and you have the means to make a quick pie, jam tarts, or quiche.

❀ MUST-HAVE KITCHEN EQUIPMENT ❀

Pocket tip 🦋

Rule of thumb: buy the best your budget allows, building a collection gradually.

It is worth investing in a food processor: a basic blade, whisk and grater are the only essential attachments, although a jug is useful for making smoothies or milkshakes. A handblender is also practical if you are pureeing food for babies on a regular basis or making soups. A breadmaker is not cheap but is worth it for fresh bread at a fraction of the price of commercial varieties and saves lugging home the loaves.

Essential
- Two saucepans: large and small
- Frying pans: large and small (pancake)
- Heavy casserole dish
- Knives: bread knife, small paring knife, large chopping knife
- Scales
- Measuring jug
- Mixing bowl
- Measuring spoons and cups

Nice to have
- Handblender
- Breadmaker
- Reusable baking sheets
- Cupcake tin

❀ FAST FOOD THAT ISN'T JUNK ❀

Sauces and marinades are the quickest way to create a tasty meal out of nothing, providing the base for pasta, risottos, soup or grilled meat and fish.

EASY CHICKEN STOCK

1. Place a roast chicken carcass in a large pot of cold water with one stalk of celery and an onion; bring to the boil and simmer for four hours, removing any scum with a slotted spoon. Allow to cool and remove any surface oil.

2. Freeze in ice cube trays and use for soups, risottos and stews.

EASY TOMATO SAUCE

Make in double or triple quantities and freeze. Add to 450g browned mince for instant (if not very authentic) bolognese, or layer with sliced aubergine and Parmesan and bake in the oven for a vegetarian supper.

With pasta, serves 4.

1. Heat 1 tbsp of olive oil and fry one chopped onion and one sliced garlic clove until soft.

2. Add one chopped stalk of celery and two to three types of vegetables (eg half a sliced sweet pepper, one peeled sliced carrot, one diced courgette).

3. Add 400g tinned chopped tomatoes, half a tin of water or vegetable stock, 1 tbsp of tomato puree, 1 tsp of sugar, 1 tsp of dried mixed herbs and a splash of balsamic vinegar. Add salt and pepper to taste and cook over a low heat for 20 minutes. Remove from the heat and blend until smooth.

Pocket tip 🦋

Adding vegetables to this easy tomato sauce is a great way of increasing your child's five a day intake. You can cook the vegetables separately and blend them thoroughly before adding to the tomato sauce — your kids will never know it contains so much goodness!

EASY CHEESEY SAUCE

Serves 2 adults or 3–4 children

1. Heat one small tub of mascarpone with 1 tbsp of hot water until the cheese has melted, but do not allow to boil.

2. Remove from the heat and stir in two handfuls of grated cheddar and $\frac{1}{2}$ tsp of English mustard.

3. Add to cooked macaroni, place in a shallow oven-proof dish and top with a handful of grated cheddar.

4. Grill until golden and bubbling.

For variety and extra flavour, add peas, ham, sweetcorn or tinned tuna along with the macaroni.

EASY MARINADE

Serves 2 adults or 3–4 children

1. Combine 1 tbsp of clear honey, 2 tbsp of soy sauce, 1 tsp of sesame oil and 1 tsp of teriyaki sauce.

2. Stir together and use to marinate two fish or chicken fillets.

3. For quick kebabs, chop the chicken or fish into chunks and place on skewers before grilling.

4. Add 1 tbsp of crunchy peanut butter and/or 1 tbsp of sweet chilli dipping sauce for a spicier sauce that goes well with egg noodles.

As a child my family's menu consisted of two choices: take it or leave it.
Buddy Hackett

'Not spag bol again . . .': five meals with beef mince

- **Bobotie**. *Soak one slice of white bread in 100ml of milk, squeeze to remove the milk and mix with the mince. Combine with one chopped onion, 75g raisins, 75g flaked almonds, 1 tbsp chutney, juice of one lemon, 1 tsp curry powder, ½ tsp of turmeric and 1 tsp of salt. Brown the mince mixture and put into a greased loaf tin. Beat two eggs with the leftover milk and pour over the meat. Bake in a preheated oven at 180°C/gas mark 4 for about 30 minutes or until set.*

- **Chilli**. *Sauté the mince and add fresh tomato sauce (see above), one 400g tin of kidney beans, rinsed, and one chopped dried chilli. Serve with rice, grated cheese and/or tacos.*

- **Nachos**. *Layer tortilla chips with grated cheese and beef chilli, grill until the cheese has melted, then add two more layers. Scatter on jalapeños and top with guacamole and/or sour cream. Eat with your fingers.*

- *Meatloaf*. Fry one chopped onion with 1 tsp of ground cumin until soft. Combine in a large bowl with the mince, one handful of fresh breadcrumbs, one beaten egg, 1 tbsp of ketchup, and optional 10 dried apricots, chopped. Add seasoning. Press into a greased loaf tin and place in a large roasting dish filled with cold water that comes halfway up the side of the tin. Cover the tin with foil and cook in a preheated oven (180°C/gas mark 4) for 90 minutes, removing the foil for the last 30 minutes. Turn out from the tin, slice and serve with couscous and a green vegetable.
- *Burgers*. Combine the mince with one beaten egg, one handful of breadcrumbs, a squirt of ketchup, one finely chopped onion and a large pinch of mixed herbs and seasoning. Shape into five patties and chill for an hour before shallow-frying in oil for five minutes each side.

❀ QUICK PICK-ME-UPS ❀

Many children prefer all-day grazing to the demands of three meals daily. So it is worth making sure that those snacks comprise a reasonably healthy mix of the recommended five-a-day fruit and vegetables, high-energy carbohydrates and protein.

Store cupboard snacks
- Dried apricots
- Breadsticks
- Rice cakes
- Crackers and nut butters
- Chopped fruit
- Cartons of fruit juice
- Popcorn
- Ice-cream cone filled with fresh fruit and yoghurt
- Cupboard trail mix: combine cereal, dried fruit, desiccated coconut, sprinkles

❂ THE ULTIMATE SNACK: ❂
HEALTHY AND EASY TO MAKE

Tea loaf

Makes about 8–10 slices

1. Soak 300g of dried fruit for at least two hours in warm strong tea.
2. Preheat the oven to 180°C/gas mark 4.
3. Drain and mix the fruit with 175g light brown sugar and two beaten eggs.
4. Stir in 225g plain wholemeal flour and 1 tsp each of baking powder, allspice and ground nutmeg.
5. Turn into a greased 900g loaf tin and bake for 90 minutes.
6. Serve sliced and buttered.

Muesli flapjacks

Makes about 16

1. Preheat the oven to 180°C/gas mark 4.
2. Mix together 150g muesli and 200g oats in a large bowl.
3. Melt 150g unsalted butter with 100g light brown sugar and 4 tbsp of golden syrup in a small pan over a low heat. Pour it onto the muesli and oat mixture. Mix well, then tip into a greased 18cm square tin and press down.
4. Bake for about 35–40 minutes until golden brown. Cool slightly in the tin, then cut into bars with a sharp knife and loosen around the edges. When firm, remove from the tin and cool on a wire rack.
5. Store in an airtight container for up to a week.

Cheese scones

Makes about 12

1. Sift 500ml plain flour with 3 tsp of baking powder and a large pinch of salt. Add 250ml grated strong cheddar cheese.
2. In a separate bowl combine 15ml vegetable oil, one egg and 125ml milk.

3. Add the wet ingredients to the dry and mix to form a dough.
4. Roll out and flatten (avoid using a rolling pin as this will prevent the scones from rising) and cut into circles.
5. Bake in a preheated oven at 180°C/gas mark 4 for 15–20 minutes.

❀ COOKING FOR FRIENDS ❀

An inevitable part of family life is having people round, often with little notice: gangs of hungry teenagers, last-minute playdates, and unexpected family lunches. It is worth stocking your freezer with garlic bread and frozen vegetables (which can bulk out a quick pasta dish or risotto). Packets of bacon or pancetta, tins of olives and anchovies, eggs and cheese, all keep a long time and can be put to a multitude of uses. Puddings can be quickly whipped up out of good-quality ice-cream, frozen summer fruits, and dark chocolate.

For guests who give more notice, look for dishes that can be made in advance and then reheated: casseroles and pies are perfect here. Starters such as antipasto or soup are hassle-free and again can be prepared ahead of time.

LAST-MINUTE WONDERS

Quick carbonara

Serves 2 generously

1. Soften one chopped onion in oil and add 1 small packet (about 70g) of chopped pancetta.
2. Meanwhile cook the spaghetti, adding 1 tbsp of frozen peas per person three minutes before it is ready.
3. Mix together one glass of white wine, one egg and one large handful of freshly grated Parmesan.
4. Drain the pasta and return to the warm pan. Quickly add the cheese and egg mixture, stirring so the egg 'cooks' in the heat. Add the pancetta mixture and serve.

Fajitas

Serves 4

1. Marinate strips of skinned chicken breast (one per person) up to four hours beforehand in the juice of one lime, three sliced garlic cloves, 1 tbsp of jalapeños and a handful of chopped fresh coriander.
2. Over a low heat, fry one 400g can of drained and rinsed pinto beans with four crushed garlic cloves and 3 tbsp of olive oil, mashing the beans slightly with a fork as they cook.
3. Stir-fry the chicken with strips of red and yellow pepper and onion.
4. Serve with the refried beans, warmed flour tortillas, grated cheese, sour cream, guacamole and salsa.

HERE'S ONE I MADE EARLIER: COOKING IN ADVANCE

Beef and Guinness casserole

Serves 4

1. Soften two sliced onions in a large heavy casserole dish until golden.
2. Toss 900g of stewing steak in 4 tbsp of seasoned flour and brown with the onion.
3. Add eight peeled carrots and two sticks of celery, chopped into large chunks, and cook for five minutes.
4. Pour 400ml of Guinness and 800ml of hot beef stock into the casserole dish.
5. Bring to the boil, then turn the heat down to low. Cover and let it simmer over a low heat for approximately two hours or until the liquid has reduced and thickened by about two-thirds.
6. The flavour improves if left for a day or two, and it will keep in the fridge for up to five days.

African vegetable stew

Serves 4

1. Fry a chopped onion with two crushed cloves of garlic, 2 tsp of ginger, and a pinch of caycnnc pepper in a casserole dish.

2. Add 1 tbsp of mild curry paste and cook for one minute.
3. Add 350g peeled and chopped sweet potatoes and/or butternut squash, one 400g tin of chopped tomatoes, two large handfuls of shredded fresh spinach or chard leaves, and 300ml of vegetable stock. Bring to the boil, then turn the heat down and simmer for 20 minutes or until the vegetables are cooked.
4. Soften 4 tbsp of crunchy peanut butter with a ladleful of hot stock and stir into the stew with one 400g tin of drained and rinsed chick peas and two handfuls of garden peas, frozen or fresh.
5. Before serving, add seasoning to taste and a handful of chopped fresh coriander. Serve with flatbread and yoghurt.

❀ COOKING WITH KIDS ❀

Weighing, measuring, pouring, tasting: many elements of cooking are educational and fun, and the best way to introduce children to a range of foods. Getting your children involved in the kitchen from an early age will teach them good habits and means they are less likely to be fussy eaters.

Falafel

Makes about 8

1. Blend one 400g can of chickpeas, drained and rinsed, in a food processor until smooth.
2. Add one crushed clove of garlic, 1 tbsp each of chopped fresh parsley and mint, 1 tsp of ground cumin, zest of half a lemon, 1 tbsp of lemon juice, and 2 tbsp of fresh bread-crumbs. Mix well.
3. Form into balls using hands, pressing the mixture so that it sticks together.
4. Place in the fridge for 30 minutes to firm up.
5. Shallow fry a few at a time in oil, for about 10 minutes or until golden.
6. Serve in pitta bread with salad and Greek yoghurt, though children may prefer them dipped in tomato ketchup.

Pizza

Makes 2 large or 4 small pizzas

1. Mix together three cups of strong white (bread) flour, one cup of water, 1 tsp of fast-action dried yeast, 1 tsp of sugar, $\frac{1}{2}$ tsp of salt and 1 tbsp of olive oil.
2. Knead until it becomes a smooth dough, adding more flour or water if the dough is too sticky or solid.
3. Cover the bowl with clingfilm and allow to rise for around 30 minutes. Divide the dough into two large balls, or four balls to make smaller pizzas; pat out into round pizza bases. Place on greased baking sheets.
4. Spread with tomato sauce or puree, sprinkle with grated cheese and decorate with a combination of the following: sliced onion, pitted olives, sweet peppers, fresh mozzarella, ham, salami, tuna, pineapple, cherry tomatoes.
5. Bake in the oven at 200°C/gas mark 6 for 20 minutes.

Pocket tip 🦋

Children love decorating their own pizzas, so you can give each child an individual pizza base to decorate. Lay out the toppings in bowls in the middle of the table, ensuring they include some vegetables, and not just cheese and meat!

All-in-one cupcakes

Makes 12

1. Combine two eggs, 125g self-raising flour, 125g butter, 125g caster sugar, and 1 tsp of vanilla essence in a bowl, and beat until smooth.
2. Fill 12 cupcake cases and bake for 18–20 minutes in an oven preheated to 180°C/gas mark 4, until the cakes are firm and golden.
3. Ice and decorate with a selection of the following: silver balls, dragées, glace cherries, sprinkles, mini-marshmallows, liquorice laces, jelly beans. Try making animal faces pigs,

mice, cats, insects caterpillars, spiders, butterflies, or flowers.

Chocolate crispie cakes

Makes 12

1. Place 200g of good quality chocolate, broken into pieces, with 1 tbsp of butter and 1 tsp of golden syrup in a heatproof bowl.
2. Place the bowl on top of a saucepan of barely simmering water (make sure the bowl does not touch the bottom of the pan).
3. Alternatively, heat the bowl in the microwave for 2–3 minutes, in short 30 second bursts, stirring each time. When almost fully melted, stir well until smooth.
4. Remove the bowl from the heat and add 100g cornflakes, stirring until they are all coated.
5. Place a heaped tbsp of mixture into each paper case and refrigerate until set.
6. Experiment by adding different types of cereal, dried fruit, mini-marshmallows, etc. Substitute dark or white chocolate for a more sophisticated or sweeter flavour.

Ten useful meals to teach your teenager to cook

1. *Scrambled eggs*
2. *Spaghetti bolognese*
3. *Baked potatoes*
4. *Leek and potato soup*
5. *Macaroni cheese*
6. *Sausage casserole*
7. *Beef chilli and rice*
8. *Tuna pasta salad*
9. *Lentil dhal with rice*
10. *Roast chicken with roasted root vegetables*

❀ PACKED LUNCHES ❀

Making a packed lunch every day that is also healthy and interesting is a headache most mothers can do without. To further complicate matters, many schools ban all nut products and anything vaguely confectionery, including chocolate spread and fizzy drinks. Keep it balanced by sticking to a general rule of one carbohydrate (sandwich or pasta), one protein (humus, cold meats, cheese, etc.) and at least two portions of fruit or vegetables. Increase the nutrition by choosing wholemeal bread or pasta. Schools that ban processed treats often don't mind homemade muffins or flapjacks, which contain less sugar than commercial varieties and can provide some much-needed energy for hungry children.

Ten ideas for packed lunches

1. *Thermos flask: baked beans, soup, smoothies, macaroni cheese*
2. *Spanish omelette*
3. *Chicken skewers*
4. *Cold sausages*
5. *Pasta salad*
6. *Pizza slices*
7. *Wraps: tuna mayonnaise, chicken salad, falafel*
8. *Pitta bread and humus*
9. *Hard-boiled eggs*
10. *Cheese scones and butter*

Pocket tip 🦋

Save a portion of food from last night's dinner to include in a packed lunch the next day. Cook extra rice or pasta and add chicken or tuna and sweetcorn to make a hearty salad.

Make a packed lunch fun
- *Pack pretty napkins and drinking straws*
- *Cut sandwiches into shapes*
- *Use muffins, pitta bread, bagels or bread sticks instead of plain sliced bread*
- *Draw faces on bananas and boiled eggs*
- *Cut fruit into bite-sized portions, ready peeled*

❀ PERFECT PICNICS ❀

Summer isn't summer without a picnic. By taking your own food you can turn an ordinary trip to the park into an event that all children love.

Do

- Raid the deli: buy a selection of cheeses and cold meats, olives, sun-dried tomatoes and speciality bread for an easy, no-preparation-required feast.
- Remember the napkins, wineglasses, corkscrew and wet wipes.
- Keep everything fresh with a cool box.
- Designate a plastic bag to be used for rubbish.
- Take portable dense cakes such as banana bread or lemon polenta cake.
- Keep it light with chilled rosé wines or real ale.

Don't

- Buy unappetising pre-packed sandwiches.
- Make food with mayonnaise, which congeals in the heat.
- Take salads that require cutlery. Stick to finger salads such as cherry tomatoes, celery and cucumber sticks.
- Leave your rubbish behind.

❁ HERBS AND SPICES, AND ❁ WHAT TO DO WITH THEM

Herbs and spices are the quickest way to lift the taste of an ordinary dish into something extraordinary, a method that other cultures – Italian, Turkish, Indian – have always known.

Herbs can be split into two varieties:

- Green and leafy (parsley, fresh coriander, basil, sage)
- Twiggy (rosemary, thyme, oregano)

To maximise their flavours, as a rough guide, add the woody, hardy type at the beginning of cooking (including all dried herbs), and the fresh ones at the end.

Classic herb flavourings

- **Gremolata**. Combine crushed garlic, lemon zest, finely chopped mint and parsley. Stir into chicken stews or add to couscous.
- **Bouquet garni**. Tie a bay leaf, a few sprigs of thyme and parsley with a strip of leek or string, and add to soup and stock, removing before eating.
- **Herb tapenade**. Roughly blend together a small bunch of oregano, parsley, three thyme sprigs, the juice of one lime, one garlic clove, 1–2 tbsp of red wine vinegar, olive oil, salt and black pepper.
- **Herb salt**. Combine sea salt in a shaker with one tbsp each of crushed dried bay leaves, dried thyme, dried rosemary, and dried oregano. Add to joints before roasting or use at the table.

There is no sight on earth more appealing than the sight of a woman making dinner for someone she loves.
Thomas Wolfe

How to . . . cook roast chicken

Very minimal preparation can provide the basis for three suppers. Buy the best quality chicken your budget allows for real flavour and good-quality meat: a decent-sized chicken is enough for two main meals and stock, justifying the extra expense.

1. Stuff the carcass with half an onion and a lemon, pricked all over with a fork. Smear inside and out with butter, rubbing salt and pepper into the skin.

2. Cook in a preheated oven in a roasting tin according to weight (20 minutes per 450g plus 20 minutes at 180°C/gas mark 4) and allow to rest for 10 minutes before serving.

3. Add chopped root vegetables around the chicken 40 minutes before it is ready for a quick roast dinner, or serve cold with bread and salad for a summer lunch.

4. Use the left-over chicken in risottos and sandwiches.

How to . . . cook roast beef

1. Use a bigger joint than you think you need: cold roast beef never goes to waste. Choose rib or beef, sirloin or topside.

2. For joints on the bone, allow 12 minutes per 450g for very rare, 15 minutes for rare and 20 minutes for well done.

3. Rub the fat with salt, pepper and dry mustard powder.

4. Preheat the oven to 220°C/gas mark 7. Place the joint on a rack in a roasting dish and cook for 15 minutes. Turn the oven down to 160°C/gas mark 3 and cook for the remainder of the time specified according to weight.

5. Remove and allow to rest for 10 minutes, covered with foil.

How to . . . make perfect roast potatoes

1. Choose a floury variety of potato such as King Edward or Cara. Peel and chop into large pieces.

2. Place the potatoes in a pan of cold, salted water. Bring to the boil and simmer for about 10 minutes or until the potatoes are soft but not cooked through (insert a knife to test).

3. Drain the potatoes (reserve the cooking water to make gravy) and return to the warm saucepan. With the lid on, shake the potatoes until their surfaces have been bashed and softened.

4. Place 4 tbsp of oil in a roasting tin and place in a hot oven (200°C/gas mark 6), carefully adding fat from the joint or

chicken if you can. Remove the tin when the fat is very hot (about five to 10 minutes) and add the potatoes, turning them so they are coated with the hot fat. Season and return to the oven, cooking for at least 40 minutes.

How to . . . make chicken soup

Renowned for its healing properties, the secret to good chicken soup is using very good stock. Ensure you always have some in your freezer.

Serves 4

1. Heat 2 tbsp of olive oil in a large stock pan, add one chopped onion and cook until softened.
2. Add two carrots, peeled and chopped, one sliced leek, one stick of chopped celery, two bay leaves and 1 tsp of dried thyme to the pan. Soften over a gentle heat with the lid on for five to 10 minutes.
3. Add four chicken leg portions, first removing the skin and any fat.
4. Pour in 1.5 litres of chicken stock. Bring to the boil then turn down the heat and allow to simmer for at least 45 minutes or until the chicken is cooked through.
5. Remove the chicken from the pot and allow to cool slightly. Strip the chicken from the bones and return it to the pot.
6. Add 50g fine noodles, vermicelli or small pasta shapes and cook for a further five minutes. Add seasoning and a handful of fresh parsley and serve.

How to . . . bake bread

Makes 1 medium-sized loaf

1. Add 2 tsp of salt and one sachet (7g) of fast-action yeast to 500g strong white bread flour.
2. Stir in approximately 300ml of lukewarm water, mixing with a wooden spoon until it forms a sticky dough.
3. Blend in 1 tbsp of softened butter.
4. Knead for about 10 minutes until the dough is smooth and not sticky.

5. Place the dough into an oiled bowl, cover with clingfilm, and leave in a warm place for at least one hour or overnight in a draught-free place or the fridge.
6. Knead the dough firmly again for a few minutes until all the air bubbles have been knocked out. Cover with a teacloth and leave for one hour.
7. Shape into a loaf and brush the top with milk to glaze. Bake in a preheated oven at 220°C/gas mark 7 for 40 minutes to one hour. Check if the loaf is baked by taking it out of the tin and knocking the base of the loaf – it should sound hollow. If it doesn't, return to the oven for another five minutes until baked through.

How to . . . bake a Victoria sponge

Makes 8 slices

1. Weigh three large eggs (with shell on) and measure out exactly the same amount of margarine, self-raising flour and caster sugar.
2. Preheat the oven to 180°C/gas mark 4.
3. Cream together the margarine and sugar either by hand or in a food processor until the mixture is pale and fluffy.
4. Add the eggs and 1 tbsp of the flour to prevent curdling.
5. Fold in the flour and 1 tsp of baking powder.
6. Divide the mixture between two lined 20cm cake tins.
7. Bake on the middle shelf for 30–35 minutes or until the centre of the cake springs back when pressed lightly (check without removing the cake from the oven).
8. Turn out of the tin and allow to cool. Sandwich the two halves together, base to base, using the very best raspberry jam, and sprinkle icing sugar on top.

Pocket tip 🦋

For a quick method of lining a cake tin, cut a square of baking parchment roughly wider than the cake tin. Fold in half, then half and half again. Cut the outside corner in a circular shape. Unfold and place in the tin. There is no need to grease the tin as well.

How to . . . ice a cupcake

1. Make eight cupcakes, using the recipe on p 13 but using muffin cases, filling them only halfway.
2. Mix 100g of sieved icing sugar with 15ml of warm water to create glacé icing. Drop in minute amounts of food colouring using the handle of a teaspoon. (Food colouring pastes give a more professional finish without diluting the icing.)
3. Fill the cake case with the icing so that it reaches the top of the paper case, with no sponge showing.
4. Substitute the water with lemon or orange juice for a stronger flavour. Sieve 2 tsp of cocoa powder with the icing sugar before adding the water for chocolate icing.
5. Decorate with silver dragées or hundreds and thousands.

How to . . . bake the perfect cookie

Makes about 12

1. Preheat the oven to 170°C/gas mark 3. Grease baking trays or line with parchment.
2. Sift together 250g of flour and $\frac{1}{2}$ tsp of bicarbonate of soda and $\frac{1}{2}$ tsp of salt; set aside.
3. In a separate bowl, combine 170g of melted butter and 300g of light brown sugar. Beat in 1 tsp of vanilla extract, one egg and one egg yolk until light and creamy and then mix in the sifted ingredients until just blended. Stir in 325g of chocolate chips.
4. Drop the cookie dough onto the prepared baking trays, allowing around 1 tbsp of dough per cookie, placing them about 8cm apart. Bake for 15–17 minutes or until the edges are lightly browned. Don't over-cook; the cookies will be soft when removed from the oven but will crisp up as they cool.
5. Transfer to wire racks after a few minutes to cool completely.

How to . . . make pancakes

Makes about 8

1. Sift 110g plain flour with a pinch of salt.
2. Make a well in the centre of the flour and break two eggs into it. Whisk the eggs, folding in the flour.

3. Gradually incorporate 200ml milk and 1 tbsp of sunflower oil, whisking until the batter is smooth.
4. Leave the batter to stand for one hour.
5. Heat a small frying-pan until it is very hot, then turn the heat down to medium. Ladle in about 2 tbsp of the batter. Tip it from side to side so that the pan is evenly coated. Cook for about 30 seconds until the bottom is golden. Flip the pancake using a palette knife, then slide it out of the pan onto a plate.
6. Stack the pancakes, adding sheets of greaseproof paper between them to keep warm while making the rest.

I got the blues thinking of the future, so I left off and made some marmalade. It's amazing how it cheers one up to shred oranges and scrub the floor.
D. H. Lawrence

How to . . . make marmalade

Makes 5lbs (about eight jars)

1. Cut 1.5kg of Seville oranges and two wax-free lemons in half and remove the pips without discarding them. Squeeze the juice into a jug. Cut out as much of the pith and flesh as possible from the peel. Place the pith, flesh and pips in the middle of a muslin cloth, gather together the ends and tie with string.
2. Slice the skin into fine shreds and place in a large, flat-bottomed pan with 4 pints (1.89 litres) of cold water, the juice and the muslin bag. Bring to the boil and simmer uncovered for approximately two hours or until the liquid has reduced by 1 pint and the peel is very soft.
3. Remove the muslin bag and drain, squeezing it to remove all the liquid. Add 450g of sugar to the pan for every pint (0.47 litres) of liquid (there should be about three pints or 1.42 litres) and stir until the sugar has dissolved.
4. Boil the mixture rapidly for about 15–30 minutes or until it has begun to set. Test this by placing 1 tsp of the liquid on a cold saucer: if the skin wrinkles when pressed, it is ready.

5. When the setting point has been reached, turn off the heat and leave to stand for 15 minutes. Stir and spoon into warm sterilised jars. Cover the tops with waxed discs and leave until completely cold. Cover with transparent discs and fasten with elastic bands.

Pocket tip 🦋

To sterilise jam jars, wash thoroughly in hot soapy water or in the dishwasher, or place in a preheated oven at 130°C/gas mark ½ for 15–20 minutes.

How to . . . make the perfect cup of coffee

1. Only use fresh, good-quality coffee beans, and preferably always grind the coffee immediately before brewing.
2. Allow 2 level tbsp per cup of coffee for a strong flavour.
3. Medium to coarse ground coffee works best in a cafetière. Use freshly boiled water and allow it to stand in the jug for three to four minutes. Stir before pushing the plunger down slowly.
4. Never reheat coffee, or let it sit on a hot plate for more than 20 minutes.
5. Warm the milk and pour it first.
6. Store coffee in a dark, air-tight bag in the fridge (not the freezer).

How to . . . make sloe gin

Sloes are the berries of the blackthorn bush, which is commonly found in English hedgerows. Sloes are blue and round, and larger than blueberries. Collect in October and November, traditionally after the first frosts.

1. Pick and freeze the fruit: this avoids having to prick it.
2. Half fill a glass container with the frozen fruit: an empty gin bottle or demi john is ideal.
3. Fill the rest of the bottle with gin, noting how much you have added.
4. For every half litre of gin add between 170g and 220g caster sugar, depending on the fruit and how sweet you like your drink.

5. Give the mixture a good shake: all the sugar will sit at the bottom due to the frozen fruit.
6. Give it a good stir every couple of days for the first week and then once a week for two months.
7. After about six months decant it into a 'nice' looking bottle. It will be ready to drink after another six months – the longer you wait the better it will be.

How to . . . make mulled wine

Christmas in a glass . . .

Serves 4–6 people

1. Wash and slice two unwaxed lemons and two oranges, leaving the peel on. Place two bottles of red wine in a large pan and bring to a simmer slowly. Do not allow to boil.
2. Add the lemons, oranges, two fingers of brandy, a small handful of cloves, a sprinkling of ground nutmeg and 1 tbsp of sugar. Simmer for approximately 20 minutes. Add three cinnamon sticks and simmer for a few minutes more.
3. Serve warm in mugs or glasses.

How to . . . make Pimms

1. Allow 50ml of Pimms per person.
2. Put it in a large glass jug and fill it quarter-full with a mixture of thinly sliced cucumber, strawberries, orange and lemon.
3. Add plenty of ice and fill to the top with lemonade.
4. Garnish with mint springs and borage flowers.

For an extra punch, add one measure of gin per person to the mix.

How to . . . make real lemonade

1. Roughly chop four unwaxed lemons and place in a food processor with 100g sugar and 500ml water. Blitz to a pulp.
2. Strain through a sieve into a jug, extracting as much liquid as possible.
3. Top up using another 500ml of water, adding ice, lemon slices and a sprig of mint.
4. Add a handful of raspberries, fresh or frozen, to the food processor to make pink lemonade.

DOMESTIC GODDESS: CHORES AROUND THE HOUSE

There is nothing like staying at home for real comfort.
Jane Austen

Small children move through the day with a long trail of dirty clothes, bits of clutter, and obscure stains travelling in their wake. And it doesn't seem to get any better as they grow into messy teenagers. Maintaining some sort of domestic order in the face of this chaos is one of the more basic responsibilities of motherhood. A clean, ordered house not only imbues a sense of warmth and comfort, but your day-to-day life will also be that much easier if the kitchen is not over-run by ants and you know where to find the sellotape. This doesn't mean being superwoman – just maintaining a healthy distance from chaos.

After enlightenment, the laundry.
Zen proverb

❀ LOVING THE LAUNDRY ❀

Laundry is a love/hate task: everyone appreciates fluffy towels and crisp clean sheets but not the pile of dirty washing and mountain of ironing that inevitably precedes them.

WHEN TO DO IT?

Traditionally, Monday was wash day—reserving the hard labour for after the day of rest. Some people still prefer to make one day a week wash day and get it all out of the way, while others opt for little and often. With small children, it is often more practical to throw on a wash every day.

Pocket tip 🦋

Loading the machine last thing at night and hanging out the clothes first thing in the morning can be a useful part of the daily routine.

Children in particular can get into the habit of putting all their clothes into the wash daily to avoid hanging them up. But jeans and jumpers can bear several outings before requiring cleaning, so check that only dirty clothes are being washed.

Eco-tip 🌱

Halve the amount of washing detergent recommended by the manufacturer—for example, use one tablet instead of the pre-packaged two.

HOW TO DO IT?

- Separate the laundry into three groups: whites, light colours and dark colours. At the very least, washing white fabrics separately avoids dingy fabrics.

- Don't overload the drum as this will prevent the machine from cleaning thoroughly.

- Wash similar fabrics together, such as woollen items or towels.

- Most machines nowadays have a handwash option for, say, woollen items, though it is never worth risking the more delicate items.

Pocket tip 🦋

Add 1–2 tbsp of washing soda (sodium carbonate) to the detergent drawer to reduce calcium deposits and also the amount of washing powder needed by up to a third.

Drying clothes outdoors is often the most effective and economical method. Tumble dryers, albeit a necessary evil in the damp British climes, use tremendous amounts of energy. Also, excessive heat damages the fibres.

How to . . . dry clothes inside

- If you have the space, a ceiling rack or Sheila Maid is a more stylish and practical alternative to plastic airers, freeing up floor space and taking advantage of the circulating warm air.

- Hanging garments correctly when drying can greatly reduce the amount of ironing needed, or even remove the requirement for it altogether.

- Garments should be snapped free of larger creases and hung as they will be worn, for example, pegged at the waist for skirts and trousers.

- Button up shirts and place on rust-proof hangers.

Pocket tip 🦋

Whoops!

If a stray red sock turns your white or light colours pink, don't panic. If the laundry is still damp, wash it again with a double dose of detergent. For whites, add 4 tsp of bleach to the detergent drawer, though avoid bleach with woollens, silk and polyester.

Shrunken jumper?

Add 2–3 tbsp of hair conditioner to a bucket of room-temperature water. Leave to soak for five minutes then lay the jumper on a clean dry towel and stretch out the fibres to its original shape, allowing to dry on the towel.

❁ IRONING ❁

Ironing is often regarded as a chore but the pile can be quickly reduced by asking yourself, 'Does it really need ironing?'. You may be pleasantly surprised as to how much of the ironing basket can be dispensed of in this way.

- If damp washing is hung out properly, snapped smooth and pegged carefully, many modern fabrics won't need further pressing.

- Removing clothes quickly from the tumble dryer, then shaking and smoothing will also get rid of most creases.

- Modern school uniforms are designed not to need ironing – likewise with some sheets, jeans and so on.

- If you are pushed for time, ask yourself whether anyone will really notice whether the children's pyjamas, the baby's vests or your jogging pants are crease-free.

- An attractive bedspread hides wrinkled sheets.

Pocket tip 🦋

Don't bother ironing socks or underwear! This might sound obvious, but you'd be surprised how many mums spend precious time on this.

However, freshly ironed shirts and bed linen do look good and feel better. So if you do want to iron these . . .

- For the most effective finish, try to do it while your cotton and linen items are still damp.

- Use a spray bottle or the steam/spray function on your iron if they have dried.

- Iron garments inside out to avoid shiny patches on delicates and woollens.

How to . . . iron

- **Shirts**. Pull the shirt tight, starting with the sleeves. Begin by ironing the cuff, both inside and out, then work towards the armhole. Iron straight across the back yoke, each front side, and finally the collar, beginning at each tip and ironing towards the middle to avoid wrinkles.

- **Sheets**. To iron flat sheets, fold into quarters and press lightly on both sides.

- **Wool**. Press the iron, rather than moving it forwards and backwards, on the wrong side of the garment or through a clean tea towel to avoid shiny patches.

Pocket tip 🦋

Keep it in perspective: there is little point being very uptight about folded clothes and hospital corners while sharing a living space with children.

De-clutter

Our houses are over-flowing with possessions and our children in particular are more materially endowed then any previous generation, and yet all this 'stuff' easily becomes a source of stress itself.

Sort out the physical mess and often the mental state will take care of itself. At the very least, the less stuff there is, the less there is to clean.

The golden rules

- Start small: desk drawers, the saucepan cupboard, the children's shoes.
- Use three boxes labelled 'Chuck', 'Maybe' and 'Keep'. Begin with the things you definitely want to throw out. Then select the items you're not sure about for the 'Maybe' box and put it away for six months; if you don't miss the items during that time, move them swiftly to the 'Chuck' box.
- Go through the 'Chuck' box and separate the junk from items that could go to a charity shop.
- Sort the items you want to keep, using the 'a place for everything, everything in its place' rule.
- Select one place to keep oft-used items—for example, a key board for keys.

Learn to recognise what is junk: old electrical items, bowls filled with random objects, anything broken, clothes that haven't been worn in the last year, odd earrings, old newspapers and unread mail, half-finished projects, unwanted gifts.

Have nothing in your houses that you do not know to be useful or believe to be beautiful.
William Morris

❄ SPRING CLEANING ❄

Although central heating and vacuum cleaners have removed the need to get down on your knees and scrub, there remains something very cathartic about a good shake-down of the entire house once a year. Break it down into manageable blocks, ticking off one task at a time, and satisfy your inner Ena Sharples.

- Put away winter bedding, heavy duvets, flannel sheets and winter coats
- Take the curtains to the cleaners
- Shake out rugs, airing them on the washing-line
- Wash floors
- Get carpets professionally cleaned or hire a carpet cleaner for the weekend
- Dust skirting boards and cornices
- Dust bookshelves
- Polish everything glass: windows, photo frames, television sets
- Empty and clean kitchen cupboards

CHORES: GETTING SOME HELP

Good habits last a lifetime and your future daughters-in-law in particular will thank you for raising tidy children.

- **Start young**. Make a tidy up session before bathtime an integral part of the day.

- **Set ground rules**. For example—pen lids must be replaced, outdoor shoes put away, and pyjamas folded under pillows.

- **Everyone helps**. Children grumble about clearing up when they didn't make the mess. You can make the point that it isn't parents who scatter jigsaw pieces or drop playdough on the floor. Make it clear that everybody tidies up, every day.

- **Show what needs doing**. Children often don't recognise toys on the floor as mess.

- **Make it easy**. Use easy-to-reach boxes—for example, one box for train sets, one for play food.

- **Reward particularly good behaviour**. Household tasks should be regarded as part of family life, not something that children are paid to do. However, extra-special effort can be recognised with sticker charts for younger children and additional pocket money for older kids.

EASY TASKS FOR CHILDREN

Preschoolers
- Picking up toys
- Putting their clothes in the laundry basket
- Laying the table

5–10 years
- Loading the dishwasher
- Washing the car
- Sweeping the floors

11–16 years
- Vacuuming
- Gardening tasks
- Taking out the rubbish

> *Everybody wants to save the earth; nobody wants to help Mum with the dishes.*
> P. J. O'Rourke

Common household stains and how to remove them

The golden rules

1. Act quickly, as dried stains are much harder to remove.
2. Don't apply hot water.
3. Blot any excess with kitchen towel.
4. Work from the outside of the stain inwards and always dab, rather than rub.

- **Blood**. Soak and rinse repeatedly in cold salty water. Wash using biological detergent.
- **Chocolate**. Soak in lukewarm water and apply a salt solution before washing.
- **Chewing gum**. Chill the garment in the freezer and chip off the hardened gum. Dab with methylated spirits.
- **Curry**. Keep the stain wet and apply glycerine before rinsing with tepid water.
- **Red wine**. Pour over white wine or mineral water and dab with a cloth Apply glycerine before washing. Never apply salt as it 'sets' the stain.
- **Felt-tip pen**. Wash and blot with cold water if the pen is water-soluble. If not, dab with nail polish remover or hair spray; wash as normal.
- **Crayon**. Freeze, then scrape off hard wax. Dab with white spirit to remove the coloured stain.

Don't cook. Don't clean. No man will ever make love to a woman because she waxed the linoleum: 'My God, the floor's immaculate. Lie down, you hot bitch.'
Joan Rivers

❀ PESTS: RODENTS, NOT THE ❀ CHILDREN

Prevention is better than cure when it comes to unwelcome guests as many infestations are difficult to clear. Pay attention to gaps in the skirting board and hot-wash bed linen regularly. Always clean up spills and store opened food packets in cupboards, using food clips and lidded containers.

- **Ants**. Pour boiling water directly onto the nest. If you can't find it, put down ant poison, which the ants will carry back to the nest.

- **Bedbugs**. Clean and change bed linen regularly and keep the areas around and under beds clear and dust-free. Bedbugs are difficult to get rid of so you will need to call in professionals.

- **Fleas**. Treat infested pets with insecticide and burn infected bedding. Use a commercial flea spray.

- **Clothes moths**. Spring clean wardrobes, dry-clean infested clothes or place in a plastic bag and freeze for 24 hours. Keep only seasonal clothes in the wardrobe, and vacuum pack the rest. Never place dirty woollens or cashmere back into a wardrobe.

- **Mice and rats**. Keep kitchen surfaces clean and all food tidied away. Block potential entrance holes with wire wool. Use humane mouse traps, baiting them with chocolate peanut bars and/or borrow a cat. Call in professionals if you suspect a severe infestation, particularly rats.

- **Spiders**. Never kill them as they eat a number of other household and garden pests. Scoop up by covering the spider with a small cardboard box and sliding a piece of thick paper underneath.

❁ PETS ❁

Pets can be a great way to teach responsibility and affection to children. However, if you are still at the baby and toddler stage it is worth seriously considering whether you need another small creature to feed and toilet train. Add to that vets bills and pet insurance, and the decision to adopt a pet is not one to be made lightly.

Cute cuddly creatures can also be the source of some unpleasant infections such as salmonella, intestinal worms and toxoplasmosis, as well as the ubiquitous flea.

UNEXPECTED PROBLEMS: PETS TO THINK TWICE ABOUT

- **Hamsters**. These are strictly nocturnal creatures so may be on the quiet side for a child who wants something to play with.

- **Rabbits**. These are surprisingly poor pets and are the animals most likely to be returned to animal centres: they don't like to be kept alone and are liable to escape on a regular basis, as well as create havoc in a garden.

- **Dogs**. These require a lot of commitment and not all breeds are suitable for family life, so consult carefully before indulging those demands for a puppy.

HASSLE-FREE 'MINI-PETS'

Okay, so an ant doesn't give out much in the way of one-to-one affection but the following can be interesting and will test out a child's willingness to take on the responsibility. Hassle-free pets include:

- Stick insects
- Goldfish
- Ant farms
- Sea-monkeys

Pocket fact 🌱

43% of the UK population owns a pet. The most popular pets are fish, followed by cats and dogs.

CARING BEHAVIOUR: TEACHING CHILDREN TO CARE FOR PETS

The benefits of looking after a pet are wide ranging and often surprising: children with pets are said to have stronger immune systems, resulting in fewer days missed at school, increased self-esteem and compassion, and they find it easier to share.

Do

- Show consideration by not handling your pet roughly as your child will imitate your behaviour.

- Teach your children that pets need 'quiet-time' and must not be constantly disturbed.

- Show your child the correct way to handle a pet–avoiding the tail of a dog, etc.

- Make your child responsible for at least one part of the pet's care–eg changing the water bowl.

PET HYGIENE

Teach your children basic pet hygiene

- Wash hands after touching all animals
- Don't let pets sleep on beds
- Don't let cats walk on tables or kitchen surfaces
- Don't allow rodent cages to be kept in bedrooms
- Keep feeding bowls away from food preparation areas
- Never allow pets to beg at the table or lick plates

Pets in the home

- Keep the house well-ventilated and encourage pets to go outside
- For dogs and cats, vacuum daily if possible, paying attention to upholstery
- Shake out a pet's bedding daily and hot-wash it weekly
- Clean cages weekly and outside if possible

❀ DECORATING CHILDREN'S ❀ BEDROOMS

Organising and decorating a child's bedroom is a tricky matter of combining fun and comfort with a high level of organisation and multi-functionality. And if your child wants wall-to-wall Barbie while you're thinking Carl Larsson, compromise is inevitable.

- **Involve your child**. If your child has some say in how the bedroom looks, they are more likely to keep it tidy and clean.

- **Choose classic**. Select furniture that will last through the years and can be put to multiple uses or moved to different rooms—eg the top of a chest of drawers can double as a changing table for a baby, and bunk beds can be split into two single beds.

- **Keep themed items to bed linen and accessories to accommodate fickle tastes**. Use large wall stickers and soft furnishings for decorative detail. Opt for a general theme, such as space, jungle, rainbows, etc, rather than cartoon characters that date quickly.

- **Use different containers to sort toys, sticking on pictures if your child can't read**. There are many cheap and stylish options available that combine for books, bulky toys and clothes.

Ten mothers in film

1.	Mrs Bates	Psycho
2.	Manuela	Todo Sobre Mi Madre (All About My Mother)
3.	Mrs Robinson	The Graduate
4.	Margaret White	Carrie
5.	Mildred Pierce	Mildred Pierce
6.	Aurora Greenway	Terms of Endearment
7.	Sophie Zawistowski	Sophie's Choice
8.	M'Lynn Eatenton	Steel Magnolias
9.	Mrs Iselin	The Manchurian Candidate
10.	Erin Brockovich	Erin Brockovich

IN THE GARDEN

There is great pleasure and satisfaction to be derived from having your own patch of green, and getting back to nature can provide a necessary counterpoint for children besieged by material goods. Even the smallest urban garden can be attractive and productive so lack of space is no excuse.

Many beginner gardeners are put off by the huge tomes of gardening advice and lists of necessary equipment; but all you really need is some compost, seeds or seedlings, and a patch of soil to plant them in. Seed packets contain all the information you need on how and where to grow. Give it a go!

❀ GROW YOUR OWN ❀

CUT FLOWERS

Wandering into your own garden and snipping off some home-grown blooms is enough to satisfy anyone's inner domestic goddess. In addition, growing flowers will brighten up your home inside and out. Bought cut flowers are often expensive and surprisingly unkind to the environment.

What to grow

- **Perennials**. These plants typically provide flowers for three to five years. They often thrive better when left alone so are perfect for the time-pushed gardener. Examples: alliums, anemones, black-eyed Susans, chrysanthemums, columbines, delphiniums, lupines, Michaelmas daisies, peonies.

- **Annuals**. Excellent value for money as one single packet of seeds will flood a flower bed with colour. Self-seeding varieties appear year after year. Sow on warm soil in drills in order to distinguish from weeds. Examples: nasturtiums, nigella, poached egg flowers, cosmos, California poppies, cornflowers, lisianthus, stocks, sunflowers.

- **Spring bulbs**. Plant spring-flowering bulbs in early autumn, though tulips need to wait until November. Be sure to plant within a week of buying them or they may sprout. Choose sunny, well-drained positions to avoid rotting. Plant bulbs two to three times their own depth and two bulb widths apart. Examples: Hyacinths, crocuses, daffodils and tulips are easy to grow and their early bursts of colour provide welcome signs of spring.

Pocket tip 🦋

The best flowers for scent: hyacinths, daffodils, nicotiana, sweet alyssum, sweet peas, jasmine, lilac, pinks, sweet violet.

Pruning

Pruning helps plants replace old, dying matter with healthy shoots, while also creating a regular and attractive shape. Prune in autumn and winter when plants are typically dormant if the climate is mild, otherwise wait for spring.

Pocket tip 🦋

Rule of thumb: Gardeners can debate endlessly the correct method of pruning roses, but a bad prune is better than a rampant rose.

- **Roses**. Prune when the plant is dormant, although this does depend on the exact variety of rose. Make 45-degree cuts about half a centimetre above an outwards-facing bud, ensuring the cut is clean and not ragged. Remove all broken, dead or dying wood and any weak branches thinner than a pencil.

- **Shrubs**. Prune shrubs after flowering in early spring. Remove old, dead wood, reducing the number of stems roughly by half. Evergreens don't need pruning.

- **Fruit trees**. Trained trees such as espaliers need pruning in late August, but free-standing trees should be left until dormant in winter. First remove any dead or diseased branches, moving on to branches that cross over each other. If the tree is already tall enough, then cut any new growth by two-thirds.

How to . . . arrange flowers

Which flowers?

Local flowers that are in season provide the best value for money and are kinder on the environment. Look out for UK-produced daffodils, tulips, hyacinths, anemones, and orchids.

What mix?

- Base the arrangement around one shade and use texture and shape to add interest.

- Use flowers at different stages of development, from closed buds to open blooms.

- Avoid combining too many varieties, which can look fussy and old-fashioned.

- Different kinds of glass containers filled with one type of flower will have a greater impact and a more contemporary feel.

- Nature likes prime numbers: choose an odd number of tall stems for a more appealing arrangement.

Getting it right

- **Vases**. Anything can be used as a vase: tea cups, jam jars, tea-light holders, milk bottles, wine glasses etc. Place single blooms in several small receptacles for an inexpensive but effective centrepiece. As a general rule, place long stems in tall narrow vases and posies of short flowers in small, round vases.

- **Preparation**. Unwrap the flowers and cut an inch off the bottom, on the diagonal. Woody stems should be bashed open to maximise their intake of water. Remove any leaves that will lie beneath the water and cut the stamen from lilies to avoid staining.

- **Arrangement**. Begin with the main flowers that will provide the body and shape of the arrangement. Fill in the gaps with the buds and half-open flowers, and finish with foliage to add depth and contrast.

- **Maintenance**. Change the water and trim the stems daily to increase longevity. Keep the vase away from direct sunlight and warm radiators.

Pocket tip 🦋

Add a quarter of a sterilising tablet to the vase water instead of flower food to keep the water clean and clear.

VEGETABLES

Surprisingly fashionable of late, growing vegetables can be one of the more satisfying aspects of gardening. If you are a novice gardener, start small. Aim to grow both what your family eats and what cannot be bought locally and cheaply. Home-grown rocket for example, provides far superior flavour and value to supermarket bagged varieties.

Seed packets always contain detailed instructions about planting, so read them carefully.

Where?

- When creating a vegetable plot in the garden, choose a sunny position with good drainage.

- An outdoor tap is particularly useful here to avoid carting heavy watering-cans in the summer heat.

- Remove stones and rubble from the soil and dig in compost or manure to increase the fertility of the earth.

- Rake the soil to a fine consistency before sowing and planting.

Pocket tip 🦋

The maximum width of a vegetable bed should be about 4ft (1.2m) in order to reach the plants without stepping on the plot.

If your soil is very poor or unsuitable, consider creating a raised bed. This will help to protect the soil and makes it easier to tend to your crops. Vegetables should be rotated according to type (root, brassicas, legumes) to avoid stripping the soil of nutrients and to avoid build-up of pests.

What?

Vegetables that are good for the novice gardener include:

- **From seed**. Peas, beans, summer squash, Swiss chard, rocket, radishes, mizuna.
- **From seedlings**. Tomatoes, peppers, chillies.
- **From sets**. Onions.

Pocket tip 🦋

Grow tomatoes, aubergines, chillies and cucumber plants in growbags on sunny patios or balconies.

HERBS

Fresh herbs are attractive and easy to produce, providing pots of flavour at a fraction of supermarket prices.

Where?

- Any well-lit, well-drained corner of the garden will do, either among mixed beds or in their own plot.

- Herbs look particularly striking in a variety of pots on a patio or windowsill.

When?

Plant in soil-based compost (as opposed to peat) and feed containers from March to October to promote leaf growth.

Pocket tip 🦋

Don't allow a herb plant to flower: this is a sign that it is completing its life-cycle. Pinch the flower off and use the plant more frequently to encourage ongoing growth.

What?

Easy herbs to grow

- **Full sun**. Bay, thyme, basil, lavender, chives, sage, rosemary, French tarragon, oregano, verbena, dill.
- **Partial sun**. Rocket, sorrel, mizuna, mustard, parsley, lemon balm and chervil.

Pocket tip 🦋

Mint (including lemon balm) can be very invasive so try growing it in a pot sunk into the ground.

Taste what you grow: herb tea or tisane

1. Take a large sprig or five fresh leaves per cup of boiled water.

2. Press lightly on kitchen towel and add to a cup or teapot.

3. Pour over freshly boiled water and cover to prevent the essential oils from evaporating.

4. Leave for five minutes and strain into a cup.

❀ GREEN FINGERS: MAKE YOUR ❀ OWN COMPOST

All good gardeners know that creating a fertile garden is really about creating good-quality soil and this is best achieved using nature's own method of recycling. Compost is produced when dead plants rot down and decompose, creating a rich earthy soil full of nutrients.

It is better to start making compost in spring, when the warm days will help rot the dead matter faster. Either make a heap in the open air or in a large plastic bin.

Pocket tip 🦋

Many councils provide free compost-making bins as part of their own recycling strategy.

HOW TO CREATE A COMPOST HEAP

- Allow at least 1sq m, driving in stakes or orange boxes to build a container.
- Cover the heap with old carpet or plastic to increase the heat and encourage the rotting down process.

What to add

Aim for a mix of all types. If your compost looks too wet, add more paper; too dry, add more green waste.

- **Green plant waste**. Grass clippings, leaves, flowers.
- **Brown plant waste**. Bark, twigs, hedge trimmings.
- **Uncooked food waste**. Teabags, fruit cores, peel.
- **Rough paper**. Newspaper, brown paper, egg boxes; preferably shredded.

Pocket fact 🌱

Never add cooked food to compost as this will attract rodents and pests.

WHEN TO USE YOUR COMPOST

The compost will take at least three months to mature and is ready when it is dark and crumbly with a sweet, earthy smell.

❀ ATTRACTING BIRDS AND INSECTS ❀
TO YOUR GARDEN

All gardens can be made more wildlife-friendly and creating a greener environment allows children to observe and learn about nature. (See p 140 for how deal with stings and bites.)

Eco tip

Encourage birds and insects into your garden: they are natural predators and will keep pests such as slugs away from flowers and vegetables.

- Put out bird feeders and boxes, hanging them away from predators such as cats.
- Refill feeders regularly as birds will come to rely on the supply. A variety of food will attract all types of birds: use unsalted nuts, seeds, and dried fruit.
- Birds need to bathe regularly to clean their feathers. A shallow bowl of water makes a useful bird bath.
- Allow one corner of the garden to become overgrown to encourage wildlife. Rotting logs are a haven for ladybirds and hedgehogs.

Common British garden birds
- House Sparrow
- Starling
- Blue Tit
- Blackbird
- Chaffinch

Pocket fact

A single bird will gulp down 500 to 1,000 insects in an afternoon.

CREATING A BUTTERFLY GARDEN

Butterflies are a source of beauty and wonder for children (and adults) of all ages. Although the UK has 58 varieties of butterflies, they are becoming increasingly rare due to a fatal mix of climate change and modifications in land management: 2008 recorded the lowest numbers of butterflies for 27 years.

Caterpillars and butterflies need host plants to lay their eggs, and nectar and water on which to feed. Plant holly and ivy in a sunny spot where they can grow tall and flower for the holly blue.

Patches of stinging nettles will attract comma, small tortoiseshell and red admiral butterflies; a source of shallow water is also necessary but a wet sponge will do.

Five plants that attract butterflies

- Buddleia
- Ice-plant (sedum)
- Lavender
- Michaelmas daisy
- Marjoram

Safety in the garden

- *Little hands that like to touch and taste are not always a sensible mix with gardens that typically contain greenhouses, ponds, animal droppings and sharp tools.*
- *Use a play-pen outdoors to contain very young children who are naturally inquisitive and lack caution.*
- *Teach your children the importance of not tasting anything without first checking with an adult, not just the obvious hazards of berries and fungi.*
- *Lock away securely all garden chemicals such as slug pellets and weedkiller.*
- *Don't leave garden tools lying around.*
- *Get children into the habit of washing hands thoroughly after playing outdoors.*

- *Fence off all ponds and empty containers of water, including paddling pools and buckets.*
- *Check for gaps in hedges and ensure that gates can be locked.*

Common UK poisonous plants

- *Lily-of-the-valley*
- *Daffodil and hyacinth bulbs*
- *Lupins*
- *Morning glory*
- *Oleander*
- *Azaleas*
- *Yew*
- *Laburnum*
- *Deadly nightshade*
- *Rhubarb leaves*

❀ GARDENING WITH CHILDREN ❀

Gardening combines many of the elements that children love most: exploring, watching things grow, and making a mess. Add a few worms, bugs and mud pies, and you have the recipe for a constant source of activity.

Introducing your children to gardening can create a passion that will last a lifetime.

WHAT TO GROW OUTDOORS

Many children enjoy growing things they can pick and preferably, eat. Fruit and vegetables thrive in pots and are ideal for small hands to poke around in without damaging the prize dahlias. It is difficult to go wrong when planting potatoes, strawberries and tomatoes for example, and even the fussiest eater should be delighted by growing and harvesting their own supper.

A lack of space need not be a restriction. Even the smallest patio or a window ledge can provide enough shelter and sun; and any old container – yoghurt pot, tin can, old tyre – can be turned into a plant pot.

Growing summer strawberries

Choose summer-fruiting plants from a garden centre and use a good, multi-purpose compost. Strawberries thrive in well-drained soil in full sun or part shade.

1. *Plant in the spring, removing the flower buds from the plants so that they concentrate on establishing roots.*
2. *Space the plants 40cm apart in rows 1m apart and water well. Alternatively, use a strawberry planter, ideal for a patio.*
3. *Mulch around plants in the ground with a thick layer of well-rotted compost or straw. This prevents weeds and keeps the earth moist, as well as avoiding soil on the fruit.*
4. *When the fruit appears, cover with netting to keep the birds away.*

WHAT TO GROW INDOORS

- **Hyacinth**. Plant bulbs in the autumn in glass or plastic containers filled with water; the bulb base should barely touch the water. Keep in a dark and cool place for six weeks or until the plant has sprouted 5cm.

- **Amaryllis**. The most impatient gardener will be satisfied by this bulb's dramatic growth and giant flowers. Plant in the autumn for spring flowers.

- **Beanstalk**. Plant a dried broad bean in a small pot of potting compost, add light and keep moist. Watch the beanstalk grow.

- **Cress**. Spread moistened cotton wool on a plate, sprinkle with a packet of cress seeds, and place on a sunny windowsill. Mix with egg mayonnaise and make a sandwich.

- **Garlic**. Plant cloves of organic garlic upright in potting compost in individual pots, 2cm deep, between October and April. Harvest when the foliage turns yellow-brown.

Growing an avocado tree

You will need:

- At least one avocado stone
- Toothpicks
- A glass jar for each stone
- Water

1. Wash the avocado stone.
2. Hold it so the pointy end is upwards; push three toothpicks around the middle like the spokes of a wheel.
3. Fill the jar with water and balance the stone on top so that about 2cm of the stone is in the water.
4. Do the same with the other stones. Place the jars in a warm spot, out of direct sunlight.
5. Be patient. A root might appear in two to six weeks, but it can take up to a year. (This is why it is best to use more than one stone.)
6. When the stem is about 15cm tall, cut it back to about 7cm.
7. Once leaves appear, transfer the plant into a 25cm diameter pot filled with potting compost.
8. Water the plant well, but allow to dry out between watering.

Windowsill salad

Lettuce, chard, spinach and mizuna are satisfyingly easy to grow indoors and may tempt a young gardener into eating their greens.

Baby salad leaves

1. Sow the seeds in potting compost and cover with a dusting of soil. Mist with water daily.

2. Keep in a warm location until they sprout and then move to a sunny window. If the plants look spindly, they need more light.

3. The greens will be ready in three to four weeks. Trim at the base, starting with the outside leaves.

❀ SEASONAL GARDENING ❀
ACTIVITIES FOR CHILDREN

SPRING

- Give each child a box or basket that they can fill with soil and plant small bulbs, flowers, and stones to make a miniature garden.

- Collect blossom, daffodils and early tulips to decorate and transform a straw hat into an Easter bonnet.

SUMMER

- Collect lavender, thyme, rosemary and flowers in a jam jar. Add water and shake. Leave for a few days to make 'perfume'.

- Select the prettiest flowers and press to preserve. Borage flowers, nasturtiums, lobelia and ferns work well.

How to . . . press flowers in a book

1. Use a large heavy book (the telephone directory is ideal).
2. Place the flower flat between two sheets of paper to protect the pages.
3. Leave at least 0.5cm of pages between each pressing.
4. Weigh the book down using tin cans and leave for two to three weeks.

AUTUMN

- Collect horse chestnut seeds and hold a conker competition.

- Plant 'prepared' hyacinth bulbs in bulb jars (see p 38) to see the roots grow and the bulb flower at Christmas.

WINTER

Collect local evergreen foliage such as holly and ivy to decorate the mantel piece and banisters. Shape wire into a circle (a wire clothes hanger will do) and weave in the foliage with ribbon to create a Christmas wreath.

4

CHILDCARE ESSENTIALS

❁ LITTLE BUNDLES OF JOY: BABIES' ❁ HEALTH AND WELL-BEING

Babies need to be loved, fed, and kept warm and clean. It is surprising how little equipment and appendages are really necessary to achieve this. Saying that, some devices do make day-to-day life with a small baby easier. But leave the musical vibrating playzones for the grandparents to buy.

> *Before I got married I had six theories about bringing up children;*
> *now I have six children, and no theories.*
> John Wilmot, Earl of Rochester

Everything your baby needs to . . .

- **Wear**. *Six babygrows, six vests, sunhat, socks, three cardigans/jumpers, outdoor suit, warm hat.*
- **Travel**. *Buggy, car seat.*
- **Sit**. *High chair.*
- **Sleep**. *Cot, mattress, two cot sheets, three blankets.*
- **Keep clean**. *Nappies, nappy sacks, wipes, cotton wool.*
- **Feed**. *If you are using formula: bottles, teats, bottle brush, steriliser, formula milk. If you are breastfeeding: breastfeeding bra, breastpads.*

Things that will make your life easier

- Sling
- Bouncy chair

- Muslin cloths
- Portable changing mat
- Moses basket
- Bath seat
- Baby sleeping bag
- Changing bag
- Monitor
- If you intend to express breastmilk: pump, steriliser, bottles, teats, bottle brush.

❋ HOW TO BATH A BABY ❋

Some babies love a bath, others will scream through every minute. Though it can form a useful part of bedtime routine, there is no requirement to bath your baby every day. 'Topping and tailing', or washing the face and nappy area with warm water and cotton wool will keep your baby sufficiently clean; indeed, too much soap and bubble bath can be harmful to a baby's sensitive skin.

Pocket tip ❧

Never ever leave your baby unattended in the bath, even in a bath seat. If the phone rings, take baby with you—so always keep a towel close to hand.

1. Gather everything you will need in the bathroom: a towel, clean nappy, facecloth, mild soap.

2. Make sure the room is warm and run the bath, adding the cold water first, until it is approximately 38°C. Newborns don't need soap but you can use a mild bubble bath for babies if you wish.

3. Fill the bath to about 10cm deep or until your baby's shoulders would be covered. It should be waist deep for babies and children who can sit up.

4. Gently lower your baby in, supporting the neck and head.

5. Wash using a soft cloth or by splashing water onto your baby, talking gently for reassurance.

6. Wrap your baby in a soft warm towel and pat dry. If he or she has dry skin or nappy rash, apply baby moisturising oil or lotion.

❀ BABY SLEEP TIPS FOR THOSE ❀ DESPERATE MOMENTS

There never was a child so lovely but his mother was glad to get him to sleep.
Ralph Waldo Emerson

- Teach your baby to wind down at night by introducing a bed-time routine as soon as possible. A calm bath, quiet story and last feed in a darkened room at a set time every day will help your baby recognise when it is bedtime.

- Keep the room dark by using blackout blinds, particularly in the summer.

- Put your baby in their cot while still awake as early as possible so they learn to settle themselves.

- Give your baby a few minutes to settle but don't leave a very young baby to cry for long periods.

- Put your pillowcase in the cot to reassure them with your scent.

- Keep one special toy in the cot that your baby will associate with going to sleep.

- There's no need to change a nappy during the night unless it is particularly soiled.

- Don't worry about every noise – it's usual for babies to make lots of squeaks, groans and sighs while sleeping.

- Try not to get irritated; this is difficult when you are sleep-deprived but a baby will pick up on your frustration and find it harder to settle.

- Get help: ask your partner to take turns with getting up in the night. If you are feeling very exhausted and stressed ask your health visitor to refer you to a sleep clinic.

❀ FEEDING ❀

Pocket tip 🦋

Many babies are reluctant to take a bottle from their mother if they have been breastfed. Ask your partner or a trusted person to try first.

How to . . . give a bottle

1. Warm the bottle by standing it in a jug of hot water. Shake to ensure there are no hot spots and check the temperature on the inside of your wrist: the milk should feel warm rather than hot.

2. Sit comfortably with your baby in a semi-upright position supported by your arm and tilt the bottle so there are no air bubbles in it. Introduce the teat to your baby's lips, allowing a few drops to fall until your baby starts to suck. Make eye contact and smile, chatting to reassure your baby.

3. If your baby won't let go of the teat, gently slide in a clean finger between the lips and the teat to break the suction seal.

4. Spluttering and dribbles of milk are signs that the flow may be too fast. If your baby is making a lot of gulping and sucking sounds, he or she may be taking in too much air, resulting in painful wind. Try different teat sizes or anti-colic teats and bottles to relieve discomfort after a feed.

5. Some babies prefer their milk sitting up and may take in less air in this way. Try sitting your baby on your lap facing out with his or her back to you.

TROUBLE-SHOOTING BREASTFEEDING

- **Blocked ducts**. Feed from the affected breast first and frequently, applying hot compresses and massaging the lump, stroking towards the nipple. This can be done while feeding. Don't ignore blocked ducts as you can develop mastitis (infection in the tissues of the breast).

- **Cracked nipples**. Ask your health visitor, midwife or breastfeeding counsellor to check if your baby is latching on properly and/or for thrush. Lanolin cream will soothe painful skin, and you can use nipple shields if you have very badly cracked nipples to allow the skin to recover.

- **Nipple pain**. Check your baby is latching on correctly. Ensure that the baby's mouth opens wide and that the bottom lip is covering more of the areola than the top lip. If your breast is particularly large or engorged, try squeezing the nipple flat to enable this.

- **Engorgement**. Express or breastfeed as frequently as possible to release the milk. Putting a green cabbage leaf inside your bra so that it cups the breast will provide relief (yes, it does). Also, spraying your breasts with warm water from a shower head will encourage let-down.

- **Mastitis**. Rest and feed as frequently as possible, starting with the infected breast first. If feeding is too painful, express to get the milk flowing, using massage and hot and cold compresses to clear any blocked ducts and encourage let-down. If the infection does not clear within 48 hours, contact your GP, who can prescribe antibiotics. Taking ibuprofen will help with the inflammation but consult your midwife first.

- **Low milk supply**. Consult with your health visitor or midwife to check whether your baby is gaining weight, which is the clearest indicator of a good intake of milk. Does he or she have five to eight regular wet and dirty nappies in one day? Do they seem contented after a feed? Look after yourself: rest and eat well. Put your baby to the breast as often as possible and express in between feeds to stimulate supply and avoid using dummies or top-up feeds: the more your baby feeds from you, the more milk you will produce.

FIVE WINDING TECHNIQUES

- **Over the shoulder**. Hold your baby up to your shoulder and rub their back.

- **Sitting up**. Sit your baby upright, cupping his or her chin in your hand so their neck is straight.

- **Along your forearm**. Lie your baby along your forearm so their stomach is pressed against your arm and swing (gently!) from side to side.

- **Cycling**. Place your baby on their back on your lap and cycle their legs.

- **Face down**. Lie your baby across your lap and rub their back with circular movements.

❂ WEANING ❂

Weaning can be one of the more confusing milestones for mums, bombarded by an overwhelming amount of advice—much of which is contradictory. Take it slowly, trust your instincts, and enjoy it as your baby discovers a whole new world of food and greater level of independence.

The UK Department of Health recommends that babies are exclusively breastfed for the first six months (26 weeks). If you feel that your baby is ready before this, talk to your health visitor.

Signs that your baby is ready for solids

- Able to hold the head up straight and can sit upright when supported
- Demanding more frequent milk feeds and seems unsatisfied afterwards
- Waking with hunger having previously slept through the night
- Birth weight has approximately doubled

Jars of ready prepared baby food are quick and convenient, particularly when out and about, but given the simplicity of first tastes, it's cheaper – and easier – to make your own purees. Make plenty in one go and freeze in ice cube trays, decanting into freezer bags. Babies like their first tastes to be wet, soft and bland: begin by introducing one vegetable at a time, mixing with baby rice to create a smooth consistency. As your baby gets used to the taste and feel of purees, combine varieties of fruit and vegetables to introduce a greater range of flavours and nutrients.

WHAT YOU WILL NEED

- **Essential**. Rubber-tipped spoons, plastic bibs, hand blender, highchair, water cup with a spout.

- **Useful**. Ice-cube trays for freezing purees, mouli grater for pureeing and removing husks from small amounts, lidded pots.

WEANING FOODS TO TRY

Five tasty purees

- Butternut squash and pear
- Apple and carrot
- Avocado and banana
- Courgette and potato
- Dried fruit compote

Five first finger foods (from six months)

- Rusks: toast fingers in the oven
- Rice cakes, unsalted
- Hardboiled egg
- Apple slices
- Carrot sticks, steamed

❂ COMMON BABY PROBLEMS ❂

Dealing with

- **Cradle cap**. It is not itchy or contagious but looks unsightly. Avoid the temptation to pick at the scabs. Massaging olive oil or petroleum jelly into the scalp will help loosen the flakes, enabling them to be brushed out. If it persists, apply a shampoo designed to treat cradle cap.

- **Jaundice**. Around half of all full-term babies will develop a yellowish tinge to their skin and/or the whites of the eyes and gums in their first week. In the majority of cases, jaundice is harmless and painless and usually goes away without intervention. Sunlight helps break the chemical down so the old remedy of leaving your baby by a sunny window still holds true. Breastfeeding frequently and on demand will also help clear it. If the jaundice does not go, your doctor may refer your baby for phototherapy. This is done in the hospital, and involves placing your baby under bright fluorescent lights for set periods of time.

- **Nappy rash**. Allow air to reach the nappy area by leaving your baby's nappy off for as long as possible, preferably overnight. Try lying them on a dry towel instead. Always apply a barrier cream such as zinc oxide cream or petroleum jelly when changing a nappy, and just use plain water and cotton wool to clean the area. If the rash doesn't clear up, consult your GP, who will check for other possible causes or may prescribe an hydrocortisone cream.

- **Colic**. This usually develops in the first few weeks and lasts for around three months, affecting otherwise healthy babies who are feeding and gaining weight well. Crying often starts in the early evening and may last for several hours: the baby will draw up their legs, arch their backs, pass wind and flush red. Though harmless, it can be very distressing for parents who are unable to soothe their newborn. Constant crying can easily become overwhelming, particularly if it is disrupting your sleep on a regular basis.

To soothe a crying baby
- Wind in different positions.
- Carry baby around in a sling.
- Give a bath.
- Offer 'white' noise from a dishwasher or washing machine.
- Take baby for a drive or a walk around the block.
- Use a dummy.
- Swaddle baby by wrapping snugly in a blanket.
- Change the teats on a bottle if you are giving formula milk.

Helping yourself

- **Take a break**. If you are very upset, leave your baby in a safe place, such as their cot, and go into another room for a few minutes where you can't hear the crying.

- **Ask for help**. Let your partner or a friend take over for an hour or so.

- **Get out**. Meeting up with other mothers can help alleviate feelings of isolation and depression.

- **Prepare in advance**. Plan for the difficult time of day, such as making the evening meal in advance, so you don't have to deal with a crying baby while cooking.

- **Consult your GP**. Your doctor can reassure you about whether there are any other possible causes for the crying.

❁ POTTY TRAINING TIPS ❁

Grandparents will swear that their prodigy were nappy-free before they could walk, but it is now generally accepted that children under two do not have the physical or mental responses to deal with using the toilet.

Children are ready to train when:

- They are able to recognise and tell you that they need the toilet.
- They are capable of waiting a short time before reaching the potty or toilet.
- They are interested in other children using the toilet.
- They are able to pull skirts and trousers up and down themselves.

Do

- Involve your child in choosing a potty and pants.

- Read children's books together that discuss potty training.

- Leave potties around the house from the age of 18 months.

- Let your child see older siblings and yourself use the toilet.

- If possible, start potty training in the summer when your child can run around without trousers/skirts or underwear on.

- Sit your child on the potty each day and give lots of praise.

- The first time your child correctly uses the potty, make a big deal of it: ring the bells, call the grandparents, crack open the champagne.

- Use a star chart with stickers and small rewards for successful potty use.

Don't

- Start too young. It is usually much easier to potty train a child over the age of two although toddlers with older siblings may be ready earlier.

- Get cross. Using the potty should be an enjoyable experience and not a source of tension. Accept that accidents will happen and clean them up without reprimand.

- Be scared to leave the house. Most children can wait up to two hours between using the loo and are often keen to use unfamiliar toilets.

- Overdo the praise and/or nagging. Your child may become resistant to using the toilet if they feel under pressure.

- Dread it. Try and make potty training a positive time for you and your child with plenty of praise and treats. Think of the benefits of not having your child in nappies.

Pocket fact 🌱
Foods that encourage constipation, so to be given in moderation, include: bananas, rice, apples, cheese, citrus juice, and fizzy drinks.

❀ GETTING OUT AND ABOUT ❀

The arrival of a baby means the end of just grabbing your clutch bag and tripping gaily out of the front door. The smaller the child, the larger the bag you seem to need for even the simplest trip to the shops.

To save time, keep a bag ready prepped with the following items:

- Three nappies
- Baby wipes
- Nappy sacks
- Portable changing mat
- Spare baby vest and babygrow
- Sunhat/warm hat depending on the weather
- Sunshade or raincover depending on the weather
- Blanket
- Purse, keys, mobile phone, travel pass, notebook

Other useful things to remember

- Use a sling or light collapsible buggy if using public transport.

- If travelling by underground, check the relevant website to see which stations have lifts.

- Be assertive and ask for help with stairs: people are usually happy to help but are often shy about offering.

- Many large shops and shopping centres have quiet rooms where you can feed in peace: often with a sink, changing mat and microwave.

❀ CHILDCARE: YOUR OPTIONS ❀

Remember that children, marriages, and flower gardens reflect the kind of care they get.
H. Jackson Brown

Organising good quality and affordable childcare is a daunting task for any mother: never underestimate how emotional and insecure you may feel about entrusting your child to someone else's care.

A myriad of options are available, and each family's needs can differ widely. So start considering your choices well in advance:

- Allow plenty of time: this could mean starting when you are pregnant.

- Ask friends for recommendations.
- Trust your gut instincts: if you are unsure about someone, say no.
- Follow up all references, preferably by phone.
- Have back-up plans in case of an emergency.
- Phase in your child's time with a carer gradually.

NURSERY

Nurseries provide an often bewildering range of childcare options from round-the-clock care for babies with the inevitable steep fees; to community nurseries, offering a few hours of structured activity for pre-school children.

Pros

- All staff should be qualified and have had a CRB (Criminal Record Bureau) check by the police.
- There is an opportunity to mix with other children.
- A range of facilities and activities are available for your child.
- Care is always available – there is no risk of your carer being ill.
- Day nurseries fit in with office hours and rarely close for holidays.
- Nurseries are required to meet set standards through Ofsted (Office for Standards in Education) inspections.

Cons

- A possible high turnover of staff.
- Less chance of consistent one-to-one attention for a small baby.
- Fees can be expensive.
- Parents have no say in the choice of staff.
- Children are not allowed to attend when ill, even with minor infections such as conjunctivitis.
- The noise and high levels of activity might not suit a quiet or shy child.
- Usually very limited flexibility when it comes to picking up times.

What to look for in a nursery

Pocket tip ❧

A good nursery will have: warm, friendly staff with a low turnover; a bright, safe environment; stimulating, varied activities; regular access to outside play.

- Check that all the facilities, equipment and toys are in good condition, clean and secure.

- What is your gut instinct: does it seem like a warm and welcoming environment? Are the staff chatty and smiling? Do the children appear happy?

- Watch the interaction between staff and children – are they engaging and nurturing the children?

- What kind of meals are offered? Is the food healthy and appealing? Are menus changed regularly? How are the children encouraged to eat?

- Visit at different times of the day: are the children allowed quiet time? How is outside play supervised?

Questions to ask

1. Can I look around the building and see the rooms where my child will be? Where is the outside play area? How often do the children go out?

2. What is the staff-to-child ratio? How much individual attention will my child receive?

3. Are there regular outings for the children?

4. How flexible are the hours? Do you offer part-time or full-time places?

5. When was your last Ofsted inspection and can I see the report?

6. How is an average day structured?

7. What is the staff turnover rate?

8. What happens is a staff member is off sick?

Pocket fact 🌱

Minimum staffing ratios:
1 member of staff: 3 children under 0–2 years
1 member of staff: 4 children under 2–3 years
1 member of staff: 8 children under 3–5 years

NANNY

Finding your very own Mary Poppins may seem like an impossible task but a dependable and enthusiastic nanny can become a welcome part of the family and a crucial element of working motherhood.

Selecting the right person depends very much on your particular needs: very young babies benefit from the patience and experience of a more mature person while an enthusiastic younger person may suit active school-age children better.

How to . . . interview a nanny

- Conduct the initial interview without the children present in order to avoid distractions.

- Ask the nanny to explain her work history up to the present day, ensuring there are satisfactory explanations for any gaps. Open-ended enquiries elicit more information than questions with yes/no answers.

- Give the nanny the chance to reveal her own opinions before expressing yours—for example, 'What are your views on dummies?' rather than 'I don't believe in dummies for babies, do you agree?'

- Ask your partner or a good friend to attend a second interview in order to get another opinion.

- Trust your instincts: no matter how great a CV looks, if something is making you hesitate, say no.

Interview questions for a nanny

- *What experience do you have with children the same age as mine?*
- *How would you communicate with a parent if you had any concerns?*
- *Why do you enjoy working with children?*
- *What do you think are your particular strengths when working with children?*
- *Are there areas of your work that you plan to improve?*
- *How might you spend the day with my child?*
- *What activities would you suggest for a rainy day?*
- *How would you discipline a child?*
- *Are you still in touch with any previous employers?*
- *What difficulties have you experienced as a nanny with parents or children and how were they resolved?*
- *How many sick-days have you taken in the last year?*

CHILDMINDER

A registered childminder (see below) provides a safe home environment with fees that are usually more reasonable than those of a nanny or a nursery.

Pros

- Many childminders offer flexible hours or will collect children from school and provide meals.
- Your child can benefit from the social interaction of being cared for within a small group of children.

Cons

Shared care typically means that a childminder cannot prioritise the needs or routine of just one child.

Childminders and the law

- *Childminders in England and Wales caring for children under eight have to be registered with Ofsted. This ensures that they have passed a CRB police check, as well as a home inspection and interview.*
- *Ofsted requires childminders to have completed first aid and childminding courses and carry necessary insurance. They often also have other childcare qualifications such as an NVQ in Early Years Care and Education.*
- *Following registration, a childminder is checked again by Ofsted every one to three years.*

What to look for in a childminder

- How many other children do they care for? How do they manage the varying needs of children with different ages?

- Does the house contain pets? Do any of the residents smoke?

- Are the home and facilities clean and welcoming?

- How does the childminder structure the day? What are the different activities? How much TV is allowed?

- What happens if your child is ill?

- Do the children have access to an outside play area or a nearby park?

Maintaining good communication

Many potential areas of disagreement can be nipped in the bud by a written contract and/or job description that is agreed with your nanny at the outset. This should contain:
- **Duties and hours required.**
- **Any special requirements**. *Babysitting, language requirements, experience with special needs, dog-walking, clean driving licence, car ownership.*

- *Payment details*. As well as salary, it should cover any extra costs associated with looking after children, such as outings and leisure activities, transport costs, phone calls, food etc. Tax and NIC (National Insurance Contributions) are mandatory: would you trust an employer who refused to cover your tax?
- *Household chores*. It is usual to expect a nanny to take responsibility for many of the chores involving the children, eg preparing meals, laundry, keeping bedrooms and play-rooms tidy. Other household chores, such as ironing, are a matter of negotiation.

Set aside time, perhaps once a month, to sit down with your childcarer and discuss any irritations before they become real problems. Use a large notebook as a contact book where the carer can describe the day's events and you can respond, hence avoiding rushed conversations at handover time.

Well begun is half-done . . .
Mary Poppins

KEEPING IT IN THE FAMILY: USING RELATIVES

Pocket fact 🌱

Grandparents provide 60% of childcare in the UK.

Pros

The advantages of using relatives are clear: someone you trust implicitly, who loves your child as a family member, and may not even require payment in exchange for childcare.

Cons

- Relying on relatives for childcare can complicate family relationships in surprising ways.

- Your mother may not take kindly to being told the best way to wean a baby when she has raised several of her own.

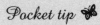

Pocket tip 🦋

Have some ground rules in place to ensure family harmony.

Do

- **Agree on basics**. Ensure you share similar ideas of suitable activities, meals, methods of discipline, toilet training and so on.

- **Pick your battles**. Decide what is really important to you and focus on this. Raise one problem at a time and discuss it in advance, particularly if you anticipate a clash in ideas.

- **Focus on the child**. 'He naps much better in his cot' sounds more positive than 'I want him to always nap in his cot'.

- **Be flexible**. Recognise that relinquishing total control of your baby's day is an inevitable part of childcare. Try to stay relaxed about relatively minor matters.

- **Build a network**. Looking after children can be isolating and monotonous. Grandparents in particular may not be aware of the many resources in your area for children. Find local playgroups, pay for a music or art class, investigate what your local library offers.

- **Review your family's needs**. Grandparents who were ideal for helping out with one small baby may struggle to keep up with three active older children. Review your childcare arrangements as your family grows in size and age.

Don't

- **Assume childcare will be free**. Your relative is giving up their time and taking on a lot of responsibility. Always offer to pay to avoid misunderstandings. If this is refused, say thank you in other ways: vouchers, a holiday, running errands.

- **Take advantage**. Try to avoid being late regularly, don't change arrangements at short notice or expect extra babysitting.

- **Underestimate how much hard work childcare can be**. You may feel jealous of the person who is spending so much time with your child, but looking after young children is not the easy option. Let your appreciation be more apparent than any resentment.

- **Disagree in front of the children**. If you have to raise difficult issues, arrange to meet separately in a quiet, relaxed setting. It is important your children know that you trust and like any individual you leave them with.

- **Allow your wishes to be ignored**. If a problem is repeatedly occurring, find alternative childcare.

❁ HOW TO DROP OFF YOUR ❁ CHILDREN WITHOUT TEARS

Your carer needs:
- At least two emergency numbers to contact you and your partner.
- A list of who may or may not collect your child.
- Sufficient milk and/or food, if it is not provided.
- Nappies and/or a change of clothes.
- Any medicines or inhalers your child may require.
- Dummies or other comforters.

Introducing your carer
- **Before**. Chat to your child about where and when they will be going, who will be looking after them and so on. There are many children's books that cover new experiences such as starting nursery and it is worth reading some with your child.

- **Beginning**. Most childcare providers suggest a settling-in period. If you can, introduce your child gradually to the new surroundings, leaving them just half-an-hour at first and building it up over a few days. Even when you are there, allow the childcarer to take charge so that your child becomes accustomed to listening to them. Always say goodbye, give a hug and a kiss, and tell your child you will be back to collect them.

- **Leaving**. If you appear confident and happy about handing over your child, he or she will follow your example. Chat to your caregiver, making it clear that you like and trust them. Keep goodbyes brief and cheerful, avoiding drawn-out hugs and tearful farewells. If your child is very upset, ask your carer to phone you in 20 minutes to check they have settled.

- **Enjoy**. Accept that it is normal to feel guilty about leaving your child. But if you like and trust your childcare provider and your child, after settling-in, appears happy there, your routine is working well. Enjoy the time to yourself while also focusing on making the most of the time you do spend with your child.

❀ GETTING THE CHILDREN SETTLED ❀

How to . . . read a bedtime story

- **How long**? It depends on the age of your child but about 20 minutes is ideal. Older children enjoy a cliffhanger ending but younger children prefer a story with resolution.

- **How often**? Young children in particular love the comfort and familiarity of endless repetition. If endless re-readings are driving you insane, insist on a new story say twice a week. An outing to the library to choose a new book makes a good incentive.

- **Get inventive**. Describe tastes, textures, sounds, colours.

- **Involve your child**. Allow your child to name the characters, describe what they look like, what the weather is like and so on.

- **Make it relevant**. Even if you're describing a world filled with pirates, dragons, magic and princesses, relate it to everyday life by giving realistic situations: boring teachers, annoying little brothers. But make sure it ends happily with all the main characters tucked up safely in bed.

Ten bedtime stories: picture books

1. *Say Goodnight*   Helen Oxenbury
2. *The Very Hungry Caterpillar*   Eric Carle

3. *Hippos Go Beserk*	*Sandra Boynton*
4. *The Runaway Dinner*	*Allan Ahlberg and Bruce Ingman*
5. *We're Going on a Bear Hunt*	*Helen Oxenbury*
6. *Maisy's Bedtime*	*Lucy Cousins*
7. *I am Not Sleepy and I Will Not Go to Bed*	*Lauren Child*
8. *Moonlight*	*Jan Ormerod*
9. *My First Oxford Book of Poems*	*John Foster*
10. *The Twelve Dancing Princesses*	*The Brothers Grimm and Jane Ray*

How to . . . stop thumb sucking

The intense need of a baby to suck diminishes from about nine months as other skills replace the comfort and stimulation it provides and so most infants will stop by themselves spontaneously. However, for some children it becomes a more persistent reflex that provides ongoing relief.

Tips on how to encourage your child to stop thumb sucking

- Note what cues prompt the habit (tiredness, shyness, etc) and provide an alternative distraction for those moments.

- Don't make a big deal about it: a child under pressure will only suck their thumb more.

- Provide an alternative comfort object such as a special teddy or blanket.

- Place a bandage on the thumb, particularly if your child sucks without being aware of it.

- Limit it to particular times and places, such as in the car or bedtime.

- Use a star chart with older children: a countdown calendar can create a deadline for stopping.

❀ CHILDREN'S CLOTHES: ❀
ESSENTIAL MAINTENANCE

Children's clothes take a lot of wear and tear but the days of throwaway clothes are thankfully long gone. Just remember the old adage that a stitch in time saves nine: it is much easier to repair a small hole than a large one, so act quickly.

How to . . . darn a sock

1. Select a cotton or yarn that matches the colour and thickness of the sock. Don't worry about an exact match as few people will see it close up.

2. Thread a darning needle with one or two strands of thread, depending on the thickness of the yarn. Don't tie a knot in the thread as that will create a bump in your sock.

3. Place the sock over a darning egg, although a smooth ball or hard-boiled egg will suffice.

4. Insert the needle above the hole and sew a few running stitches to secure the thread.

5. Make a large running stitch across the hole and repeat back and forth until the hole has been closed up with parallel stitches.

6. Now repeat the rows of stitches across the original stitches, weaving the needle in and out.

7. Fill in any gaps with more weaving and running stitches until the hole has been completely filled.

How to . . . patch a hole on an elbow or knee

Iron-on patches only offer a quick fix as they are attached by adhesive that won't survive regular washes.

Turn a sewn-on patch into a fashion statement by choosing a contrasting fabric or recycle a favourite old garment.

1. Select the patch, checking it first for size and colour-fastness. Pin it in place over the rip, positioning the pins near the edge of the patch.

2. If using a sewing machine, select a medium-width zig-zag stitch. Choose a thread that matches both the garment and

the patch, if you wish the stitches to be as invisible as possible (choose a contrasting colour if you wish to make the patch a feature). Slowly stitch the entire circumference of the patch.

3. If sewing by hand, thread the needle, choosing double or treble thickness if using a heavy fabric such as leather or tweed. Tie off one end of the thread in the patch. Make small straight stitches all the way around the patch, placing the stitches close together. If patching an elbow, blanket stitch adds a professional decorative touch.

4. Make a couple of stitches on the back of the fabric to secure the yarn and tie off.

5. Remove the pins, and admire your handiwork.

How to . . . sew on a label

This works particularly well for socks and towels.

1. Fold the label in half so that it forms a loop.

2. Sew the joined ends to the garment using double thread in the needle.

3. Six stitches should be sufficient.

If you have children of different genders, choose a neutral colour with only your surname so they can share labels.

To save the amount of labels needed, order the surname to be written twice so each label can be cut in half and used for two garments.

How to . . . sew on a button

1. Thread a hand-sewing needle with a long length of thread, doubled-up and knotted at the end. Insert the needle into the fabric so that the knot will not be visible from the front.

2. Make a couple of stitches where the button is to be placed to secure the thread. Centre the button on top of the stitches.

3. Bring the point of the needle up through the centre of the button and back into the fabric.

4. Slip a toothpick, needle, or pin between thread and button to help form the shank. Make three or four stitches through each pair of holes.

5. Bring the needle and thread to the back of the fabric. Remove the toothpick, needle, or pin.

6. Wind the thread two or three times around the button stitches to create the shank.

7. Knot the thread through the threads attaching the button to the garment and cut it.

8. For a button with four holes, repeat the above steps for the other two holes.

9. Don't over sew the button: too many threads look untidy.

How to . . . knit a scarf

1. You will need: one ball of double knitting yarn, one pair of knitting needles (the yarn instructions will specify the correct gauge), scissors.

2. Casting on. Make a loose slip knot with the end of the yarn and place it on one needle, then tighten it; place that needle in your left hand (assuming you are right-handed). Take the other needle in your right hand. Place the tip of the right-hand needle and insert it into and through the loop on the left-hand needle, so that it points away from you. Grasp the yarn (which is attached to the ball) in your right hand. Wrap it around the tip of the right hand needle clockwise and pull that needle back, keeping the loop of yarn wrapped around it. Slip the loop onto the left hand needle. The left hand needle should now have two stitches on it.

3. Cast on 30 stitches.

4. Knitting the scarf. Hold the needle with the stitches in your left hand. Grasp the length of yarn in your right, along with the other needle. Insert the tip of the right hand needle into and through the first stitch on the left hand needle. Wrap the

yarn in your right hand up and around the tip of the right hand needle. Draw the tip back and through the loop, keeping the loop of yarn on the point and also slip off the stitch from the left hand needle. There should now be one stitch on the right hand needle and 29 stitches remaining on the left hand needle. Continue knitting until the row is complete and all the stitches are now on the right hand needle. Turn that needle round so that it now becomes the left hand needle. Repeat the previous row until the desired length of the scarf has been finished. Leave sufficient yarn for casting off.

5. Casting off. Knit two stitches on a new row. Using the point of the left hand needle, lift the first stitch on the right hand needle up and over the second stitch and off the needle. Knit one more stitch and again lift the first stitch up and over the second stitch and off the needle. Continue until there is only one stitch remaining on the right needle and none at all on the left. Cut the yarn, leaving a tail of 10cm and thread this yarn through the remaining stitch, taking it off the needle and pulling tight.

Ten mothers in history

1. Medea
2. Eleanor of Aquitaine
3. Anne Boleyn
4. Mary Wollstonecraft
5. Queen Victoria
6. Mrs Beeton
7. Emmeline Pankhurst
8. Rose Kennedy
9. The Queen Mother
10. Michelle Obama

FUN WITH THE CHILDREN

❀ MESSY PLAY ❀

Creating chaotic fun is essential for children learning to explore and understand their world, as well as for improving physical skills and developing their imagination.

Do

- Let them explore. The aim is not to 'make' something.
- Go outdoors as much as possible to cut down on the mess.
- Use an old adult T-shirt fastened behind with a bulldog clip to protect clothes.

MESSY IDEAS

- **Gloop**. Mix cornflower and water until it binds. Place in a shallow tray and let your child get stuck in. Add rice or lentils to vary the consistency.

- **Painting**. Use an old roll of wallpaper and unroll it across the floor. Paint the bottom of feet or wellies and walk across. Roll marbles or string dipped in paint. Cut potatoes in half and then cut out shapes to make potato prints.

- **Playdough**. Mix together one cup of water, one to two heaped cups of plain flour, one cup of salt and two teaspoons of cream of tartar. Add food colouring and glitter as required. Wrap in clingfilm, keep in the fridge and replace regularly.

- **Chalk**. Let your child draw on the patio and outside walls. Give them a big paintbrush and a bucket of water to wash it off.

- **Water**. Fill a washing-up bowl and add bubbles and a variety of containers or plastic toys. Put in shells and stones to create a natural 'seascape'.

Pocket tip 🦋

Wary of the mess? Sit very young children in the bath to paint (while empty!) or use special bath crayons.

ART AND CRAFT IDEAS

It is very tempting for mum to step in and add the finishing touches but it is the process rather than the end product that's the fun bit, so try to stand back. Craft helps your child's creativity and concentration and can provide a welcome counterpoint to hours of television. It need not be expensive: many discarded household items can be recycled and put to creative use.

Craft cupboard essentials

- **Button box**. Snip spare buttons from clothes and keep in a jar. Use for making patterns, or to add detail to craft projects.

- **Plain flour**. Use to make playdough, paper glue and papier mâché.

- **Paper plates**. Make masks, flowers, faces, clocks, paint on food.

- **Old catalogues, magazines**. Cut up and use in collages.

- **Stickers**. Bulk-buy packets of stars and dots from stationers to make cheap and mess-free decoration.

- **Wallpaper offcuts**. Buy bin-ends for metres of drawing and painting.

Saltdough ornaments

1. Mix together two cups of flour, one cup of salt, and one cup of water.

2. Knead until smooth.

3. Roll out on a floured surface and use cutters to make shapes or roll into sausages that can be coiled. (Don't forget to make a hole using a straw if you want to hang them up.)

4. Bake in the oven at 200°C /gas mark 5 for one hour or until dry (it will depend on the thickness of your shapes).

5. Allow to cool before painting.

6. Coat with acrylic varnish if you wish to keep them a long time.

Eco-tip 🌱

To make your own glue, put one cup of water and one cup of plain flour into a saucepan. Stir until smooth. Add two more cups of water while bringing the mixture to the boil; keep stirring. Remove from the heat and allow to cool. The glue is perfect for paper projects, but make a new batch for each project as it works best when fresh.

Collage

- You will need old clothing and seed catalogues, old magazines, postcards, junk mail, sequins, buttons, stickers and natural objects, eg shells, feathers, glue.

- Cut or tear out pictures from the catalogues and magazines. Items of clothing and pictures of flowers work well. Arrange them in piles according to their colour or shade.

- Pictures to try: self-portrait, under the sea, bouquet of flowers, a city skyline.

Junk modelling

- You will need an assortment of empty cardboard boxes, cardboard rolls, egg boxes, scraps of fabric and wrapping paper and white PVC glue or sticky tape.

- Get sticking – let your child have free rein to make what they want, although you could give some ideas such as: castle, rocket, robot, flower, bed, mermaid, sun, snail.

Rubbings

- Place a coin or anything with a raised surface (embossed wallpaper, bark, leaves) under a sheet of white paper and use a wax crayon or soft pencil to rub over the top.

- Experiment with different shapes and textures (for example, oak and birch work better than pine) and make patterns with the different shapes.

One egg carton

- **Bee**. Cut out a two-cup section from the box and fold it inwards so the two rims meet. Glue together and allow to dry, trimming any rough edges. Paint on black and yellow stripes. Cut out wing shapes from greaseproof paper and add antennae, legs and eyes using pipe-cleaners.

- **Bouquet of flowers**. Cut out several cups from the box. Cut into the cup to make the petals – try different shapes, eg pointy (tulip), rounded (rose), thin (daisy). Paint and decorate as desired, using strands of wool to make the stamens. Paint craft or lolly sticks green and cut out paper shapes for the leaves and stems.

- **Animal nose mask**. Cut out a one-cup section from the box. Measure a piece of elastic around your child's head plus 5cm. Using scissors, poke two small holes either side of the cup and string the elastic through, securing with a knot. Use what ever craft supplies you have to make an animal nose: add pom-poms, pipe-cleaners, dots and stripes to make freckles and whiskers.

Craft ideas for older children

- Flower press
- Papier mâché
- Knitting/sewing
- Tie-dye
- Air-dry clay

How to . . . teach a child to tie shoelaces

Pocket tip 🦋

Use different coloured shoelaces so it is easier to tell the left lace from the right.

1. Show your child how to make an X with the two ends of the shoelace.

2. Put one end of the shoelace through the X and pull tight.

3. Make two long 'bunny ear' loops: form an X with them.

4. Put one through the bottom part of the X and pull tight.

Practise using a skipping rope: the larger scale is easier.

Ten mothers in art

1	La Pieta	Michelangelo
2	The Madonna of the Pinks	Raphael
3	Arrangement in Grey and Black: the Artist's Mother	James McNeill Whistler
4	The Bailie Family	Thomas Gainsborough
5	Mother and Child	Dame Barbara Hepworth
6	The Mother	Pieter de Hooch
7	Motherhood	Pablo Picasso
8	The Cholmondeley Ladies	Unknown
9	Mother and Child	Mary Cassatt
10	Portrait of the Artist's Mother	Vincent van Gogh

❀ THREE SCIENCE ACTIVITIES ❀

GROW CRYSTALS

You will need two jam jars, bicarbonate of soda, saucer, a length of wool and two paperclips.

1. Fill the two jam jars with hot water and stir in about 5 tsp of bicarbonate of soda (until no more will dissolve).

2. Place the jars in a warm place, either side of the saucer.

3. Cut a 1m length of wool and attach a paperclip to each end of it; place one end in each jar so the paperclip rests on the bottom.

4. Leave the jars for seven to 10 days without moving them. Crystals will emerge and grow along the wool; columns may form between the wool and the saucer.

What is happening? The wool soaks up the solution and; the water evaporates, leaving the bicarbonate of soda crystals.

MAKE A SUNDIAL

Pocket fact 🌱

The earliest known surviving sundial is an Egyptian shadow clock of green schist dating from around 800BC.

You will need a stick, playdough, stones or chalk and a clock.

1. Begin in the early morning. Place the stick upright in the playdough in a sunny spot on the lawn or pavement.

2. Throughout the day, mark where the shadow falls at each hour using the stones or chalk.

3. Try to mark 12 hours, e.g. 8am to 8pm (it may have to be completed over two days).

What's happening? The earth moves around the sun at a constant speed and so for thousands of years people and animals have been able to use the sun to tell the time.

FOAMING VOLCANO

You will need a small plastic bottle, vinegar, washing-up liquid, red food dye, bicarbonate of soda and tissue.

1. Decorate the bottle as a volcano or monster or dragon.

2. Half fill the bottle with vinegar.

3. Add a squirt of washing-up liquid and a drop of the food colouring, swirl the bottle to mix and place in a large baking tray.

4. Put a heaped teaspoon of the bicarbonate of soda into a small square of tissue and pinch and twirl the ends together.

5. Place the tissue into the bottle.

6. Sit and wait for the foam to emerge.

What's happening? The vinegar (acid) and bicarbonate of soda (alkali) mixed together create carbon dioxide, a gas which reacts with the washing-up liquid to make foam.

How to . . . teach a child to fly a kite

1. Choose a wide open space away from pylons, buildings and trees: the beach is ideal.

2. Have your child hold the string in one hand and the main body of the kite in the other hand, outstretched in front and above their head.

3. Once the kite begins to lift in the air, quickly let go and let loose as much string as possible.

4. If there is very little wind, run with the kite for lift off. Remove kite tails or anything else that will drag. Make the kite as light as possible.

5. If there is plenty of wind, tug the line with a pumping motion and let it out more. This works if the kite is dive bombing; if the kite has already crashed, fasten a tail to create drag. This adds stability, especially in high wind.

❀ MOTHERS AND DAUGHTERS: ❀ TIME TOGETHER

As children

- Organise your family photos together
- Teach her one of your skills: knitting, DIY, a musical instrument

- Start a mother–daughter book club
- Do a 'first' together: buy her first pair of earrings, first haircut at a hairdressers
- Choose each other's outfits for the day

As adults

- Take afternoon tea at a nice hotel
- Catch a matinee
- Visit your childhood home
- Go to a day spa
- Take a course together: learn a language or new skill

How to . . . tie a French plait

1. Divide the hair into about five layers from the top of the head to the base of the neck.

2. Separate the top layer into three parts. Cross the sections over each other as for a normal plait once only (left section over the middle, then right section over the middle).

3. Divide the second layer into two sections. Take the left section and add it to the left section of the first layer.

4. Cross the combined section over the middle section.

5. Repeat with the right side.

6. Continue in this way until all the layers have been incorporated in to the plait.

7. Finish by plaiting the hair that is left in the normal way and fasten with a bobble.

❀ MOTHERS AND SONS: ❀ TIME TOGETHER

As children

- Make a scrapbook together: record a holiday or family history
- Teach him your favourite recipe
- Go to see your son's sports team play
- If you can play an instrument, learn a duet
- Plant a vegetable patch together and watch it grow

As adults

- Plan a walking weekend
- Teach him to drive
- Select a book for each other to read
- Learn the same sport: fencing, tennis, golf
- Listen to each other's favourite music and compare notes

❁ FAMILY CARD GAMES ❁

Old Maid

Number of players: 2 or more

1. Remove one queen from the pack. Deal the rest of the pack evenly.

2. Each player removes all the pairs (two cards of equal value, eg two fives) from their hand.

3. Draw a card from the hand of the person to your left. If it makes a pair, remove it from your hand. All the players repeat this in turn.

4. Continue until all the pairs have been removed. The person holding the remaining queen or 'Old Maid' is the loser.

Cheat

Number of players: 3 or more

1. Deal out the entire pack evenly. Use two packs for five or more players.

2. The aim is to get rid of all of your cards by discarding them face down onto a pile in the middle, while calling out what they are (for example, 'three kings' or 'one seven').

3. The first player begins with their choice of cards and the second player follows by discarding cards of a value one higher or lower than the first (eg a two or four to follow a three), stating what they are as they are placed face down. Aces can be played high or low.

4. Other players can dispute the cards before the next person takes their turn by calling out 'Cheat!': a correct challenge means the player picks up the discard pile; an incorrect call means the challenger picks up.

Go fish

Number of players: 2–6

1. Deal five cards to each player and leave the rest face down.

2. The first player asks another player for a card or a particular rank (eg a king or a seven); note: they must already hold at least one card of that value.

3. If the other player cannot comply, they answer 'Go fish' and the player who made the request must pick up a card from the central stack. If they have the card, they must surrender it to the player; that player then keeps requesting cards from other players until someone tells them to 'Go fish' and the player to the left takes the next turn.

4. When a player has collected four cards of the same rank, they have a trick, which is then placed on the table.

5. If a player is left with no cards they must pick up a card from the central stack. The game is over when the central stack is finished. The winner is the person with the most tricks.

PIG

Number of players: minimum 4

1. Remove four cards of the same number or suit from the deck for each player – it doesn't matter which. Set aside the rest of the deck and use only the sets removed for the game.

2. Shuffle and deal the cards to all the players. Each player should have four.

3. The aim is to get four matching cards. Once the dealer says 'Go!', each player must quickly choose one card they don't wish to keep and put it face down on their left hand side.

4. Each player picks up the card the person to their right has laid down.

5. Another card is chosen to pass to the left when the dealer says, 'Go!' Keep doing this until someone gets four matching cards.

6. As soon as someone gets four matching cards they must put their finger on the tip of their nose. After seeing that player with their finger on their nose, everyone else must put their finger on their nose as well.

7. The last person to put their finger on their nose earns a P. You leave the game when you have earned all three letters P–I–G by being the last person to put your finger on your nose three times.

8. The winner is the only one in the room who isn't a PIG.

Beggar my neighbour (strip the jack naked)

Number of players: 2 or more

1. Deal out the entire pack evenly. Each player places their pile of cards face down in front without looking at the cards.

2. Each player takes a turn to flip over the top card on their pile and place it on a middle stack.

3. If the card is a number card, the turn passes to the left. If it is a picture or an ace, the player to the left must pay a penalty from their hand, turning over one card at a time and placing it in the central stack. The penalties are: jack, one card; queen, two cards; king, three cards; ace, four cards.

4. If the penalty cards are all numbers, they get placed face down at the bottom of the central stack. If a picture or an ace card is revealed, the original player wins the stack.

5. The game ends when someone has won all the stack.

Variations can be incorporated: eg seven means player to the left forfeits a go; a red ace means next pay card doesn't count.

Ten rainy day activities

1. **Make a tent.** Use chairs, blankets, duvets and pillows, and camp out in your sitting-room.

2. **Have a bath.** All get in the bath together, with lots of bubbles and plastic toys.

3. **Kitchen drawers.** Have a clear out — go through all the saucepans, Tupperware, wooden spoons and let the children help.

4. **Shoe shop.** Line up all the shoes and play shop, not forgetting receipts and bags.

5. **Hide the spoon.** Hide it in the sitting-room and let the children find it.

6. **Indoor picnic.** Blanket on the floor; serve tea as a picnic.

7. **Make a band.** First make the musical instruments: shakers (bottles filled with lentils or rice), tambourines (paper over tins), guitars (shoe boxes with elastic bands wrapped round); now sing along to your favourite songs.

8. **Puppet show.** Make puppets from socks, attaching buttons for eyes.

9. **Home cinema.** Draw the curtains, make popcorn and put on your favourite DVD.

10. **Go out.** Put on wellies and waterproofs, take umbrellas and splash in puddles.

How to . . . teach a child to ride a bike

Children either learn to pedal first (using stabilisers) or balance first (without stabilisers or pedals). There is no correct method.

Pocket tip 🦋

Using stabilisers feels easier but it tends to be slower in the long run.

- Practice on a wide grassy expanse.

- Make sure your child wears a bike helmet. If they are particularly unconfident, kit them out in knee pads, elbow pads and wrist guards.

- Practice putting on the brakes first so your child knows how to stop.

- The stabilisers should feel wobbly, with a tilt from one wheel to the other: the back wheel needs to maintain traction in order for the brakes to be effective.

- Wait until your child can confidently steer and/or pedal first, then gradually raise the stabilisers up so the bike becomes increasingly unstable.

- Hold onto your child's shoulders rather than the seat or handlebars.

- Begin on a slight downhill so your child gets used to the feeling of moving while balancing.

- Graduate to a flat surface and start letting go.

- Don't surprise your child by letting go, otherwise they may lose trust and start looking over their shoulder, unbalancing themselves.

❀ PERFECT DAYS OUT ❀

The perfect day out is often the most surprising: a long-planned trip to a theme park can mean hours of queues and expense while a last-minute outing to a new park might be novelty enough for a young child. A child who travels mainly by car may love a train ride or even a circular bus route.

Most visitor attractions now make an effort to cater for family visits with baby-changing rooms and cafés. Look for places that offer both indoor and outdoor facilities given the unpredictable nature of the British climate. It need not be expensive, particularly if you pack a picnic and stay away from the gift-shop: national museums, the parks and the beach are thankfully free.

Places to visit

- Farms—city or working
- The beach
- Museums and galleries
- Parks
- Stately homes and castles
- Garden centres
- Aquariums and sealife centres
- Boat trips
- Zoos and wildlife/wetland centres
- Swimming pool/lido

What to take: babies and toddlers checklist

- Nappies
- Wipes
- Nappy bags
- Portable changing mat
- Milk
- Snacks
- Change of clothes
- Cagoules
- Sunhat
- Suncream
- Small toy/colouring books and crayons

Bored in the park?

- **Hold a mini-sports day**. Invite some friends and take along basic sports equipment such as balls, skipping ropes etc. Organise races and keep score, giving younger children a head start.

- **Teach your children some of the games you used to play as a child**. Hop-scotch, skipping games, rounders.

- **Have a teddy bears' picnic**. Go down to the woods with teddies and picnic.

- **Take a camera**. Let your child make a record of the trip out (disposable single-use are ideal here).

- **Find the oldest tree**. Date a tree by measuring round the trunk, about 1.5m (4ft) up from the base, avoiding any bits that stick out. Approximately every 2.5cm of width is one year's growth. Divide the number of centimetres by 2.5 to calculate the approximate age.

French cricket

The origins of this classic park game remain obscure but seem to have nothing to do with France.

You need a cricket bat (though any sort of racket can be improvised with), a tennis ball and at least three players.

1. *One person begins as the batsman. A crease is drawn by marking a circle of arm's length diameter around the batsman with the bat.*
2. *Everyone else is a fielder and can stand anywhere around the batsman.*
3. *One fielder is the bowler and stands in front of the batsman, approximately 5m away.*
4. *The batsman is not allowed to move their feet, nor touch the ground with their hands; he or she is only allowed to turn to face the bowler.*
5. *The wicket is the batsman's legs. The batsman is bowled out if the ball hits their legs or the ball is caught by a fielder.*
6. *The fielder is not allowed to move until the ball has been bowled.*
7. *If the batsman misses the ball, they must play the next ball without turning to face it. The ball is always bowled from where it ended up after the previous bowl.*

❀ PLAYDATE PROTOCOL ❀

Love them or hate them, playdates soon begin to loom large in a child's everyday life. Negotiating this new responsibility can be tricky territory for parents and every mother can tell horror stories about the Child Who Wouldn't Leave or the Boy Who Bit the Cat.

Don't feel pressured to make playdates too soon. Children under two play alongside rather than with other children, hence meeting up is more an excuse for the adults to have a chat and a coffee. For parents of older children playdates can be a godsend, providing free entertainment for an afternoon.

If you're hosting

- Check whether the child has allergies or a special diet.
- Take a contact number in case of emergencies.
- Keep it small: one child is enough and avoids pairing off.
- State the house rules, eg no shoes indoors, no jumping on the sofa.
- Turn off the TV and computer games: keep them for post-playdate wind-down.
- Limit the play area to avoid children rampaging through your bedroom. Make it clear which rooms they can play in.
- Keep younger siblings out of the way: don't allow toddlers to spoil older children's games.
- Have some healthy snacks for when tiredness or bad temper sets in.
- Start a clean-up 15 minutes before the pick-up time.

Pre-school children

- Arrange a set pick-up time: one to two hours is enough for pre-schoolers.
- Check whether the child needs help with the toilet.
- Put away any particularly favourite toys to avoid issues over sharing.
- Small children need constant supervision: toddlers paired up can create a whole heap of trouble. At the same time, stand back: unless fisticuffs are flying, try not to intervene in their play.
- Be realistic: it is normal for toddlers to show clingy behaviour, to refuse to share, and to have tantrums. If fighting begins,

bring out an activity they can do alongside each other: a small craft pack is ideal.

If your child is the guest

- If your child is under four it is usual for the parent to stay, unless you know the other family well.

- If you are staying, check whether it is okay to bring younger siblings.

- Suggest a first playdate in the afternoon or morning and not over a mealtime.

- Don't be too overt regarding food likes and dislikes: children are often much more willing to try new foods at other people's houses.

- Cancel the playdate if your child is ill, no matter how inconvenient.

- Be on time to collect: ring ahead if you're going to be late or early.

- Don't hang about: make sure your child quickly puts on shoes, coat and leaves promptly.

- Be polite: check that your child has said please and thank you.

❁ CHILDREN'S PARTIES ❁

Planning a children's party should be fun and stress-free. If the mere idea of organising hordes of hyperactive kids fills you with dread, don't do it: outsource the whole thing to a playcentre or offer your child a special daytrip as an alternative. Begin by considering your budget and what facilities are available: outdoor parties mean less mess but back-up plans are necessary in case of bad weather. Hosting a party at home or sharing with another birthday child can cut down on costs.

Pocket tip 🦋
All children don't necessarily want a big party. Some may even prefer to spend the day quietly just with family.

Party alternatives

- A trip to the theatre or cinema
- Day out to a farm or aquarium
- Sleepover
- Pottery café session

Planning

- **Double up**. Sharing a party with a friend cuts down on the cost and the hassle.

- **Choose a theme**. Children love planning the tableware, invites and decorations. Now is not the time to be tasteful!

- **Involve your child . . .** Anticipation is half the fun for children. Let them have a say in the menu, writing the invites and choosing the games.

- **. . . but have the final say over invites**. Children's friends change day-to-day so don't let them exclude anyone on a whim.

- **Shop online**. Save time and use the internet to buy party bags, prizes, decorations and food.

- **Provide shelter**. Prepare for very hot weather or sudden showers with gazebos in the garden.

- **Get help**. Rope in as many people as you can: childless friends and grandparents are particularly useful here. Borrow a friend's nanny or pay nursery nurses to help out. Offload your own children the day before and/or the morning of the party to enable you to prepare in peace.

Food

- **Keep it simple**. Now isn't the time to perfect your mini-Pavlova recipe. Children rarely eat much at a party so stick to a few finger foods or old favourites.

- **Make it fun-sized**. Cut out sandwiches into small shapes, chop up fruit, and use the smallest cake cases for a child-sized feast.

- **Relax standards**. It's not a party without chocolate but bear in mind that handfuls of lollies and jelly sweets will create a roomful of hyperactive children. Squash is fine but litres of fizzy pop are probably best avoided.

- **Use disposables**. Paper plates and cups can be quickly tidied away.

- **Make it in advance**. Individual boxes make party tea very simple for younger children. Fairy cakes and birthday sponge can be baked and frozen well in advance. Use frozen pastry to make jam tarts. Make sandwiches in the morning and wrap in clingfilm to keep fresh.

- **Limit the sugar**. Avoid a menu that means children bingeing on sugar and additives. Offer plenty of fruit and avoid bowls of sweets. Save chocolate for the party bags and prizes.

- **Cater for adults**. A few grown-up snacks such as olives will suffice. Cold drinks are easier than making multiple cups of tea. Pimm's goes down particularly well at a summer party.

Party food checklist

- Sandwiches: Marmite, cream cheese, ham, jam, cucumber (not all together!). Use different types of bread and/or flour tortillas rolled up and include salad.
- Crisps
- Cheese cubes
- Cucumber sticks
- Cherry tomatoes
- Chopped fruit: grapes, blueberries, strawberries, pineapples
- Cocktail sausages
- Fairy cakes
- Crêpes: buy them ready-made. Add chocolate spread and roll up

Activities

- Face-painting
- Temporary tattoos
- Craft table: colouring-in, sticking, collages, mask-making
- Piñata
- Dressing-up box

Games

- Pass the parcel
- Pin the tale on the donkey/tiara on the princess/eye-patch on the pirate
- Musical chairs
- Musical statues
- Sleeping lions
- Scavenger hunt
- Hide the spoon
- Duck, duck, goose

PARTY THEMES

Theme: Pirate

Invite: A rolled-up message inside a empty milk or water bottle.

Food: Cones of children's magazines filled with fish fingers and chips.

Games: Pin the parrot on the pirate's shoulder; pass the cannonball, treasure hunt; walk the plank.

Cake: Treasure chest: scoop out a square cake and fill with chocolate coins and sweets.

Decorations: Inflatable crocodile or parrot, pirate flag bunting, eye patches for guests.

Theme: Princess

Invite: Royal scroll invite, tied with red ribbon.

Food: Everything pink: fairy cakes, ham sandwiches, bread sprinkled with hundreds and thousands, sparkling juice in (plastic) champagne flutes.

Games: Pass the slipper, pin tiara on the princess, decorate paper crowns, build a castle using sugar cubes, icing and sweets.

Cake: Castle: use two square cakes, one as the base, slicing the other to build towers and turrets. Hold together with icing and straws.

Decorations: Tissue flowers, glitter, pink balloons, tulle swags tied with ribbon, confetti.

Theme: Fairy

Invite: Magic wand: cardboard stars dipped in glitter and tied with ribbon to balloon sticks.

Food: Butterfly cakes, fairy fruit wands (fruit skewers on dry spaghetti), fairy dust sandwiches.

Games: Fairy scavenger hunt, pin the star on the wand, fairy tag (one fairy has 'fly' and 'freeze' wands).

Cake: Fairy garden: place fairy figurines on a cake decorated with green grass icing and sweetie flowers

Decorations: Create a fairy grotto using fairy lights, tulle, flower garlands and paper butterflies.

Theme: Space

Invite: Star stickers on black card, silver pen to invite trainee astronauts.

Food: Star-shaped sandwiches, blue jelly, flying saucer sweets.

Games: Use giant planet and star shapes to play musical chairs. Foam rockets: write each child's name on a rocket and see who can fire it furthest. Build a rocket (junk modelling).

Cake: Moon: bake a domed cake, decorate with grey icing and crushed biscuits for a rocky surface, add plastic astronauts and the US flag.

Decorations: Hang planet and rocket shapes from the ceiling. Use a revolving star light/glitter ball. Black and silver star balloons.

Theme: Beach

Invite: Cardboard sunglasses with invite written on the back.

Food: Hot-dogs, ice-cream cones, star(fish)-shaped biscuits.

Games: Beach balls, make a sandcastle, Punch and Judy show.

Cake: Beach: blue jelly for sea, crushed biscuits for sand. Add fish jelly sweets.

Decorations: Bunting and deckchairs. Sand pit and paddling pool.

Theme: **Teddy Bear's Picnic**
Invite: Written copies of the *Teddy Bears' Picnic*. Request that each guest brings a bear.
Food: Finger food in baskets served on a blanket on the floor
Games: Prizes for the oldest/silliest/best-dressed, etc bears.
Cake: Bear: use two round cakes adding fairy cakes to make the ears and paws, decorate with brown icing and chocolate buttons.
Decorations: Hang flowers and butterflies from the ceiling. Add as many teddy bears as you can find.

Ten fancy dress ideas

1.	*Christmas Tree*	*Pin baubles and tinsel on a green dress and pop a star on a hairband.*
2.	*Harry Potter*	*Spectacles, scar, wizard hat and cloak.*
3.	*Little Red Riding Hood*	*Red cloak, basket, cakes, gingham napkin.*
4.	*Pirate*	*Kerchief, eye-patch, striped top, shorts, cutlass.*
5.	*Alice-in-Wonderland*	*Blue dress, white pinafore, hairband with bow, striped tights, toy white rabbit.*
6.	*Ladybird*	*Red dress with black spots added, black net wings, deely-boppers.*
7.	*Witch*	*Green face, black cloak and hat, broomstick, stuffed cat.*
8.	*Cat*	*Black leotard, black tights, tail, ears.*
9.	*Spider*	*Black leotard, two pairs of black tights stuffed to make legs and attached. Net between the legs to make the web.*
10.	*Superhero*	*Cape, eye mask, bright home-made logo stuck on t-shirt.*

Practical tips for parties

- Make it clear on the invite whether siblings are included.

- Save opening presents for post-party wind down over the next few days, so you can keep track of who gave what, and your child will appreciate the presents more.

- Bubble machine, balloons and bunting create a party atmosphere.

- Keep a big bowl of small prizes handy to placate upset children.

- Wrap a couple of prizes spare in case an extra game of pass the parcel is needed.

- Have some idea of the running order, eg tea half-way through, games before.

- Delegate tasks: one person to make drinks for the adults; one person to run the games; two people to organise the party tea.

- Keep a list of who gave what as your child opens the presents for the thank you cards.

Alternatives to party bags

As the number of parties increases, so will your child bring home a small mountain of party streamers, bouncing balls and packets of Smarties. Why not be a bit more creative, and save yourself some money . . .?

- Buy multipacks of books and divide them between the guests.

- Balloons: attach to a stick to make them more of a present.

- Slice of birthday cake.

- Homemade sweets and/or biscuits wrapped in clear bags and tied with ribbon.

- Something crafty the child has made at the party (e.g. a bracelet).

- Each child brings an individually wrapped present that is put into a Lucky Dip bucket. Each child selects something to take home.

- Packet of seeds and plant pot.

- Take a Polaroid of each guest and attach to a balloon.

Pocket fact 🌱

A survey by Tesco revealed the average spend per party bag is now a whopping £7.48. More plastic and sweets than you know what to do with!

❁ SLEEPOVERS ❁

Having friends to spend the night is now an event in its own right: a US import that is becoming increasingly common in the UK. It is easy to turn a sleepover into a special occasion and it provides a less disruptive alternative to hosting a party. For a very exceptional sleepover, check out alternative venues such as nearby museums, aquariums and theme parks.

Whether or not you allow mixed sex sleepovers depends on your relationship with your child, their age, maturity, and how well you know their friends. If boys and girls are staying over, ensure that their parents are aware of the arrangements.

FUN IDEAS THAT WON'T SEND THEM TO SLEEP

- Decorate the bedroom with fairy-lights and supply torches.
- Stock up on junk food: popcorn, pizza, ice-cream, hot chocolate and marshmallows. Now is not the time for a health drive.
- Only invite children you know well.
- Let your child choose the DVDs but avoid horror films if you want anyone to sleep: a book of ghost stories read by torchlight is fun and less traumatic.
- Beauty supplies such as face masks and manicure sets go down well with girls.
- A Polaroid or video camera is good to record the event and provides entertainment.
- Don't forget breakfast supplies: croissants, juice, pancakes, bacon.

❁ TEENAGE PARTIES ❁

Parents will long for the simple days of jelly and ice-cream when faced with the prospect of hosting a house full of teenagers intent on partying. Few teenage guests have much regard for someone else's house and in these days of Twitter, Facebook and texting, hundreds of uninvited guests is a real possibility. Renting a location for the event can cut down on many of these problems but if that is not an option, take some sensible precautions.

If you're having it at home

- Issue written invites specifying there will be no entry without one.
- Greet guests yourself: teenagers are more likely to behave better if they know there is an adult around.
- Set ground rules: which rooms are out of bounds, no smoking in the house etc.
- Better safe than sorry: hide valuables, breakables and the drinks cabinet; roll back rugs and lock bedroom doors.
- Remain unobtrusive: your children will not forgive heavy-handed parenting.
- Provide plenty of food – Mexican or pizza is ideal.
- If alcohol is allowed, supply alongside plenty of soft drinks.
- Warn the neighbours and set a time, such as midnight, when the music must be switched off.

Teenage party themes

- Talent contest
- Beach barbeque
- Mexican
- Jamaican
- Hollywood
- James Bond

PLANNING AN 18TH OR 21ST PARTY

Parties celebrating an 18th or 21st birthday are less popular nowadays but it is still a rite of passage that often coincides with school or university graduation. It can be a great family occasion if teamed with, for example, a 50th birthday celebration, where both sets appreciate the mix of old and young.

- Collect lots of photos of the birthday child over the years: get baby photos made into coasters and posters to decorate the venue.

- Circulate a guest book for people to write their dedications.

- Before the day, ask family members and close friends to write letters to the birthday child about what makes them special.

- Create a graffiti wall: put up large sheets of blank paper, supply marker pens and let guests scrawl messages.

- Give out disposable cameras for guests to record the event.

- Hire a bartender to ensure that drinks are replenished and to keep a check on underage drinking.

- Provide a build-your-own dessert bar with a choice of ice-cream, sauces and sprinkles.

❁ PRESENT DRAWER IDEAS ❁

Having small children means years and years of party invites. Create a drawer or box in your house to store any unwanted presents in and stock up in the sales to ensure there is always a gift to hand. Books, craft kits and art supplies make ideal gifts for children of both sexes and a range of ages. Don't forget to bulk-buy wrapping paper and cards.

Pocket tip 🦋

If the child is a family member, a contribution towards ballet or swimming lessons can be a welcome alternative to yet more presents.

Perfect presents for a new baby

- Lullaby CD
- Hand-knitted blanket
- Charm bracelet (add a charm every year)

Classic books to give young children

- *Winnie-the-Pooh*, AA Milne
- *Hans Christian Andersen Tales*
- *Milly Molly Mandy* stories, Joyce Lankester Brisley
- *Peter Rabbit*, Beatrix Potter
- *Alice in Wonderland*, Lewis Carroll
- *Complete Nonsense*, Edward Lear

Older children

- Dressing-up clothes
- Craft kits
- Theatre tickets
- Children's suitcase
- Musical instrument
- Globe

Teenagers

- Instant camera
- Tickets for a festival
- Electric guitar and lessons
- Magazine subscription
- Lava lamp
- Telescope

How to . . . wrap a present

1. Remove any price labels.

2. If the present is an odd shape, place in a box.

3. Place the present on top of the unrolled wrapping paper. Cut to size, checking there is sufficient paper to cover the box, including enough to overlap slightly.

4. Place the present upside down in the centre of the paper.

5. Wrap the two longer lengths of paper around the gift. Fold the longer edge over itself so the cut edge of the paper is hidden.

6. Use double-sided sticky tape for a very neat finish.

7. At the end of the box, fold the corners in to make a triangle. Fold the tip of the triangle over to make a straight edge and tape in place.

8. Take a long length of ribbon and place the present in the middle. Wrap the two ends up the side of the box so they meet and cross in the centre of the top of the parcel; twist them 90 degrees around each other and take the ends back to the bottom of the box. Tape the ends in place. Use the remaining length of ribbon to fasten a bow where the ribbon crosses on the top of the present. Score the edge of a scissor blade along a length of ribbon to make it curl.

❊ HOLIDAYS: HAVING A WELL ❊ DESERVED REST

TOP TIPS FOR TRAVELLING WITH CHILDREN

By car

- Take advantage of your children's natural sleep patterns: set off at bedtime or just before naptime, although make sure the driver isn't too tired.

- See the journey as part of the adventure rather than just getting from A to B and build in extra time for picnics and stop-offs. Check the route for local parks and child-friendly places to eat.

- Keep a bag of emergency items in the car: wet wipes, spare nappies, change of clothes, bottle of water, dry snacks, first aid kit, blanket, torch, loose change. Take a spare plastic bag for rubbish.

- Avoid car sickness by encouraging your children to focus on sights outside of the car rather than inside. Dry crackers can help with nausea.

- Audio book CDs can be a godsend for older children, particularly if they have their own CD/MP3 players. If your journey is very long, forget the parenting manuals and get a portable DVD player.

- For young children, pack an individual bag of small cheap toys and wrap them up individually. Dole them out every half-hour. Packs of stickers, crayons and colouring books are ideal.

- Attach pocket holders to the backs of seats so your child can store and reach their books etc, without you having to pick them up all the time.

Five fun car games

- **Guess who**. *One person thinks of a family member, friend, or character from television or a book. Everyone else takes it in turns to ask questions with yes/no answers, eg do they wear glasses? The winner is the first person to correctly guess who it is.*

- **Counting cows**. *Decide on a destination where you will stop counting. Count the number of cows you can see out of your window. The winner is the player with the highest number when the destination has been reached. Go back to zero if you pass a cemetery on your side of the road. If there aren't any cows, count phone boxes or caravans.*

- **A is for apple**. *Starting with A, each person must try to be the first to spot and name three objects starting with that letter. The winner of each round chooses the next letter.*

- **Fizz buzz bang**. *Go round the players taking turns counting to 100, beginning with one. Every time you reach a multiple of seven, substitute the word 'Fizz'. On the next round substitute multiples of five as well with 'Buzz' and on a third round, substitute multiples of three with 'Bang'. If someone forgets or makes a mistake, start again from one.*

- **Scavenger hunt**. *Type up a list with your children beforehand of at least 20 things to spot during the journey.*

> *For example: someone wearing a hat, a bird of prey, a red letterbox, a tow truck, a blue Mini, a person singing in their car, and so on. Distribute a copy to everyone and work in teams if the children are very young.*

By plane

- Prepare your child for the trip by looking at picture books and discussing what to expect. Give tips on how to behave as well as instructions as to what to do should they get separated from you.

- Plan with your partner beforehand who is responsible for what at the airport, including individual children and travel documentation.

- Allow plenty of time at the airport. If your children are at the runaway-toddler stage, use a child safety harness as your hands will be busy with luggage and documents.

- Take your child to the bathroom before boarding in case of delay on the runway; airport loos will be more spacious and cleaner than those on the plane.

- Time your baby's milk, either breast or bottle, for take-off and landing to help with the changes in air pressure. Encourage older children to swallow: drinks or sweets to suck will help with this.

- Sit your child away from the aisle, preferably next to the window, where they will be away from other passengers and can look at the view.

- Pack plenty of snacks and drinks: don't rely on what the airline provides.

- Produce one toy at a time, every half-hour. If you have an MP3 or portable DVD player, now is the time to indulge their use.

- Ask staff to warm milk or baby food well in advance of when you need it: most planes don't have a microwave and items will be heated by standing them in hot water. Check the temperature very carefully as it is often very hot.

PAIN FREE PACKING

- **Write a list**. It makes packing more efficient and means you are less likely to leave something behind.

- **Think ahead**. What will the weather be like? Do the children need casual clothes or something smart for a special occasion? Are there laundry facilities at the holiday destination?

- **Plan for delays**. Pack extra nappies, wipes, milk, snacks and toys in hand luggage. Take cartons of formula milk and ready sterilised bottles.

- **Rent what you can at the destination**. Car seats, buggies, travel cots, towels.

- **Let your children take the weight**. Children love having their own suitcase—just make sure it's wheeled. If it also doubles up as a seat, so much the better.

- **Pre-holiday research**. Research online to find out what brands are available in the country you are visiting as nappies etc often have different names in other countries.

- **First aid kit**. Take a holiday first aid kit containing plasters, baby paracetamol and/or ibuprofen, calamine and after-sun lotion, antihistamine, wound wash, sterile dressings and antibacterial hand gel.

Pocket tip 🦋

Tape a piece of paper to the inside lid of your suitcase with details of where and when you are staying in case your luggage gets lost. Try not to include your home address, and use your work contact details if possible.

Useful extras

- Clothes pegs: use to peg up blankets as black-out curtains.
- Ultraviolet (UV) shades and mirror for the hire car.
- Washing powder.

- Mattress protector: a child is more likely to wet the bed in an unfamiliar place.

- Scrapbook and glue: get your children to create a record of their holiday, adding photos when you return home. Perfect for 'What I did in the holidays' school projects.

Snacks for travelling

Use small Tupperware boxes or zip-lock sandwich bags. Take a small cool bag to keep drinks fresh and never underestimate how much water you will need.

- Boxes of raisins
- Rice cakes
- Breadsticks
- Cereal bars
- Popcorn
- Dry Cheerios
- Yoghurt tubes (freeze beforehand to keep them fresh)
- DIY trail mix: combine nuts, raisins, Smarties, Cheerios, banana chips, pretzels
- Cheese biscuits

KEEPING YOUR KIDS SAFE AWAY FROM HOME

Relaxing in the sun is an integral part of holidays but letting your guard down completely can have unfortunate consequences. Follow some basic guidelines to keep everyone safe and healthy:

In the sun

- Keep children out of direct sunlight when the sun is hottest—between 12pm and 3pm.

- Babies under six months should not be exposed to the sun at all; bear in mind that most suncream is not suitable for very young children.

- Dress your family in long-sleeved, loose-fitting clothes: dark colours with a close weave offer maximum protection. If your child is in and out of water, use all-in-one sunsuits that provide UV protection.

- Children should wear a sunhat with a wide brim that shades the ears and neck as well as the face.

- Apply suncream that protects against both UVA and UVB rays frequently, paying particular attention to the face, shoulders and neck.

- Encourage your children to wear sunglasses as soon as they are old enough but check they are 'BSS' marked rather than purely decorative.

- Use a closely-woven, opaque UV sunshade in the car to protect from heat and UV rays.

On the beach

- Teach your child to swim between the red and yellow flags if the beach has lifeguards, as this is the patrolled area.

- Children should always swim alongside an adult and never venture further than knee-deep in to the sea by themselves.

- Never dive into the sea as it is very difficult to gauge the true depth.

- Children's inflatables should be secured with a line held by an adult.

- Arrange a meeting-place in case your child gets separated from you; a beach shop or lifeguard station are ideal.

- Be aware of tide times, particularly when exploring caves, coves and rock pools. Incoming tides are very fast and can quickly cut off parts of the beach.

In the pool

- Never leave children alone or near water, even for a moment. Very young children should never be further than an arm's length away from an adult in the pool.

- Check that the pool has a secure fence around all sides, with a self-closing gate and latch that a child cannot reach or unfasten.

- Keep a phone and rescue equipment (such as a long pole with a hook, and a life-buoy) near the pool.

✿ PLAYING A MUSICAL INSTRUMENT ✿

Playing a musical instrument can be a very rewarding hobby and a good alternative activity for a child who isn't interested in sport. Here are some useful points to bear in mind when introducing your child to music:

- Offer very young children a selection of percussion instruments (tambourine, bells, maracas). Put on music CDs and get them to tap along to the beat.

- The recorder is an ideal first instrument for school-age children.

- Make sure the instructor is fun: often children's enjoyment of a subject depends almost wholly on how interesting or effective the teacher is. Find someone who specialises in teaching children; don't pay for dull or uninspiring lessons.

- Let your child choose their instrument: rent or borrow first to avoid an expensive investment.

- Learn alongside your child. Make music part of your family life: take your children to concerts, listen to music radio, discuss your music preferences.

- Piano teaches timing, notes, chords and music theory and is a fantastic all-round instrument for any child. An orchestral instrument offers many social opportunities and an alternative activity if your child is not sporty.

- Children often find playing an instrument fun at first but the novelty wears off about two to three months into the lessons. Encourage them to stick with it.

6

MONEY MATTERS

❁ LOOKING AFTER THE PENNIES: ❁ HOUSEHOLD BUDGETS

Knowing how to budget is a life-skill that no one should be without. Taking control of your finances after years of carefree spending can come as a shock, but the daily expenses of a growing family easily spiral out of control at a time when every penny is needed most.

The first step is to take an honest look at the household expenditure. Check old bank statements and spend at least a week or preferably a month writing down everything you spend. Use a spreadsheet to plot the following:

WHAT'S GOING OUT . . .

- Mortgage, rent council tax, utility bills, school/nursery/childcare fees, insurance, car, mobile phone, landline and broadband, television licence and subscriptions.
- Food, clothes, transport, petrol, going out, hobbies, gym.
- Holidays, Christmas, birthday parties, dentist and opticians, vet fees.

WHAT'S COMING IN . . .

- Salary
- Benefits: child benefit, tax credits, income support
- Interest and dividends from savings and gifts

> *Pocket tip* ❧
>
> *Once it is apparent where the money goes, it will be clearer where savings can be made.*

❀ SPRING CLEANING YOUR FINANCES ❀

It is alarmingly easy to over-pay on almost every aspect of household finance, purely through lethargy and a lack of awareness. Break down the household expenses into manageable chunks and aim to revise one bill a month: there are many websites that list the cheapest options for a variety of everyday expenses in minutes. Within six months, you could be saving a significant amount of money.

- **Revise your mortgage**. This is likely to be your biggest debt so check that your current provider still offers the best deal.

- **Cut utility bills**. Switch to the cheapest provider and opt to pay by direct debit for further savings.

- **Renegotiate mobile phone and/or broadband rates**. If your contract is nearing its end, network providers will often slash monthly rates to keep your custom. If you are an infrequent user, a pay-as-you-go phone is invariably cheaper.

- **Don't overpay for insurance**. Many people pay out automatically for insurance provided by their mortgage providers or brokers. Shop around for cheaper alternatives. Don't automatically renew travel insurance until you actually need it. Pay upfront rather than in installments to avoid additional charges.

- **Check current account rates**. The days of loyalty to your high street bank are long gone. Shop around for the best rates of interest and free overdrafts.

- **Pay down debt**. Interest rates on credit cards are usually far higher than the interest paid on savings. Using your savings to clear outstanding debt will save money in the long-term.

- **Claim back bank charges**. Apply to have penalty charges on your bank accounts and credit or store cards repaid.

- **Use ISAs**. If there is spare cash doing nothing in the current account, save up to £3,000 a year in a tax-free savings account.

Swap to save money . . .

- **Premium brands for own brands**. *Try for a month and see where savings can be made without compromising quality.*
- **Clutter for cash**. *Go online and check out Nearly New sales, Freecycle, Preloved.com, Gumtree and eBay to turn unwanted goods into profit.*
- **Your house for a holiday home**. *Arrange a house-swap for a free holiday.*
- **An insulated mug for shop-bought lattes**. *Make your own coffee.*
- **Tupperware for ready meals**. *Use up leftovers and cut down on waste.*

❁ POCKET MONEY ❁

There is no 'correct' amount of pocket money: teenagers in particular are experts at feeling hard done by and there will always be at least one of your child's peers who receives more than they do. Get some consensus right from the start as to what the pocket money is expected to pay for and how extra cash can be earned.

Pocket tip ✤

Be consistent and agree on the ground rules with your child.

- Ask around your friends and children's classmates to see how much they receive but don't be overly influenced: every family manages it differently.

- Let your children spend (or waste) their money as they choose.

- Encourage savings – open a bank account or give a younger child a piggy bank. Remind them to save in advance for special events or holidays.

- Make sure that all parents and grandparents are agreed on the amount: it is tempting for non-resident parents, for example, to compensate for separation or bereavement by giving extra cash.

What pocket money might be used for

- Transport costs
- Sweets and snacks
- Magazines and books
- Toys
- Clothes other than school uniform
- Christmas and birthday presents for other people
- Mobile phone credit
- Going out costs, such as cinema and concert tickets
- School supplies, such as stationery
- Toiletries and make up

What you need to agree with your child

- Can it be supplemented by doing extra chores around the house?

- When is it due for review? Is there an automatic raise every birthday?

- Is part of it earmarked for savings? What happens to additional money, such as birthday gifts?

- Are they allowed to borrow in advance? What is the limit on this?

- Can it be withheld as punishment for bad behaviour?

- Anything they can't buy with their pocket money–eg you may wish to stop young children from spending it all on sweets.

❂ HOW MUCH TO PAY A BABYSITTER ❂

Do

- Ask around locally as rates vary a lot, depending on where you live.

- Expect to pay more for a trained nanny than a local teenager.

- Pay extra if your children will need feeding or putting to bed.

- Be generous with a good, reliable sitter so they prioritise your requests.

- Provide drinks and snacks and access to the television and/or internet, but not your phone. If the babysitter will be there before 5pm, leave a meal.

- Offer a lift or walk the babysitter home, or pay for a taxi.

- Provide a bed if you are going to be out until the early hours.

- Leave very young babies only with experienced or mature sitters.

How to . . . set up a babysitting circle

1. Enlist six to 12 friends who live locally.

2. Distribute 15–20 tokens each (cardboard circles will do).

3. Charge one token for before midnight, two for after midnight, a Saturday night, or if the children have to be fed/put to bed.

4. Circulate a list of participants detailing names, addresses, children's ages, bedtime routines, house details (how the television works, etc), emergency numbers, special require-ments (if there are pets, etc).

5. Allow members to contact each other directly to make arrangements.

❁ SAVING FOR YOUR CHILD'S FUTURE ❁

The benefits of putting away money for your child are obvious: even a modest monthly saving can provide the deposit for a first flat or funds for higher education if invested carefully over the years.

Key points

- Start early: earn interest for longer.

- Use cash accounts for small gifts, and encourage your children to save.

- The long-term aspect of children's savings helps mitigate the risk of volatility in the stock market. Look for low-cost pooled investments which provide access to a wide spread of shares and bonds.

- Take advantage of tax planning opportunities to maximise interest rates.

Bank accounts

- Children's saving accounts offer higher levels of interest–although they also often carry restrictions, such as upper age limits or maximum deposits per month.

- Children have the same personal tax allowance as adults, but as long as the total interest from the savings account falls within the personal tax allowance, there will be no tax charged.

- Ask for form R85 when opening the account to ensure that any interest is paid without the tax being deducted automatically.

Children's trust funds (CTFs)

- Children born on or after 1 September 2002 receive a £250 voucher towards starting a savings and investment account.

- The account belongs to the child and cannot be touched until the child turns 18.

- The government gives each child a further £250 when they turn seven.

- Families on low incomes receive an additional £250.

- Up to £1,200 can be saved in a CTF a year, in addition to government contributions.

- The usual regulations whereby parents pay tax on interest of more than £100 arising on capital they have given to the child (the 'settlement rules') do not apply.

- Your child is not liable for tax on any of the income from their CTF savings and investments, including dividends, interest and bonuses. Your child does not have to pay tax on capital gains arising on their CTF investments.

- The income and capital gains from a CTF account do not have to be declared in a tax return; in fact, you don't need to tell the tax office that your child has a CTF account.

- If the full £1,200 limit is not used in one year, the unused amount cannot be carried over to the following year.

Three types of CTF accounts

- *Savings account are very secure but typically offer limited returns.*
- *Shares accounts are riskier as they are dependent on the performance of the market; however, they usually a offer good return over a long period. The accounts charges are a percentage of the value and will vary.*
- *Stakeholder accounts invest in the stock market but spread the risk over a number of companies. Once your child turns 13, the money is moved to less risky investments. Charges are limited to no more than 1.5% a year.*

Points to consider

- What is the rate of return on the account?

- How risky is the investment? More risky investments give a greater return but increase the chance that all or some of the money may be lost.

- Does your family have any ethical or religious requirements regarding its investments?

- Do you prefer to pay in money over the counter or online?

❀ HOW TO WRITE A WILL ❀

One of the most important tasks that parents can do is to make a will. According to the Law Society, one in three people die intestate and risk donating a large portion of their estate to the taxman or to unwelcome beneficiaries: it is a common misconception, for example, that the surviving spouse automatically inherits everything.

Pocket fact 🌱

It is particularly important to draw up a will if you and your partner are not married: the law does not recognise common-law spouses as equivalent to married couples or civil partners.

Why make a will?

- Avoid unnecessary complications and expense for your family at a time when they are grieving.

- Ensure that your assets benefit exactly whom you choose.

- Provide for extended family and friends who are not covered legally: this includes step-children.

- Allow tax planning to avoid excessive inheritance tax.

What should your will include?

- A description of all assets, property, cash, pensions, insurance policies, shares, and personal possessions.

- The people whom you wish to benefit from your estate, including any charitable bequests.

- The names and details of two trusted people who will act as your executors to ensure the terms of the will are carried out correctly.

- Details of who will act as guardians of your children in the event of the deaths of you and your spouse. You may also wish to state how their education will be funded and at what age you would like them to access any trust fund.

Make it legal

A valid will must be made:
- *By a person aged 18 years old or over.*
- *Voluntarily and without pressure from any other person.*

- *By a person of sound mind—that is, fully aware of the nature of the document being written or signed, and aware of the property and the identity of the beneficiaries.*
- *In writing.*

It should also be:

- *Signed by the person making the will in the presence of two independent witnesses.*
- *Signed by the two witnesses, in the presence of the person making the will, after it has been signed by that person. The witness or spouses of the witnesses cannot benefit from a will.*

Do

- Obtain independent, professional advice: consult a solicitor, particularly if your estate is complicated, involving multiple properties, a business or foreign assets.

- Update it following a change in circumstances: the birth of a child, divorce, moving house and so on.

- Outline personal wishes, such as funeral arrangements or individual bequests of special items.

- Check the law for the jurisdiction where you live: for example, Scottish inheritance law differs substantially to that in England and Wales.

- Make 'mirror' wills: if you and your partner have identical bequests, it is cheaper for a solicitor to draw up near-identical wills.

- Store it safely: make copies and ensure that your executors and family know where they are. Never hide a will.

7

EDUCATION

❀ WHAT TO LOOK FOR IN A PRIMARY ❀ SCHOOL

If there were no schools to take the children away from home part of the time, the insane asylums would be filled with mothers.
Edgar W. Howe

Sending your precious first-born off to be educated by strangers is one of the more daunting aspects of parenthood. Visit each school that you have shortlisted and meet the head teacher: schools are living environments with their own unique characters and what looks ideal on paper may disappoint in reality. Chat to local parents but don't allow other people's opinions to influence you unduly: the needs and beliefs of each family are different and your idea as to what constitutes a good education may vary widely from that of your neighbour's.

Information you need from your local authority

- What schools are in your area
- Criteria for allocating places
- Deadline and procedure for applications
- What happens if your school is oversubscribed

The needs of your child

- Does your family have specific religious or cultural beliefs? Is English the second language at home?

- Special needs: does your child require particular attention or assistance? How would the school manage this?

- Personality: perhaps your child is very shy or especially able? Would your child require small class sizes or more one-to-one attention?

Visiting the school: questions to ask

- **Atmosphere**. Is it welcoming? Do the children appear happy and engaged? Are the teachers open and enthusiastic? Are there examples of work and art up on the walls?

- **Facilities**. How is the school equipped for IT, sports, music, and outside play? Where do the children eat their lunch? Are hot school dinners provided?

- **Route to school**. How long will it take? Will your child be able to walk or cycle safely? Are there friends locally who can share the school run?

- **Class size**. How big are the classes? How many classes are there in each year? How many adults are present in the class-room? Does the class remain the same as it moves up the school?

- **Curriculum**. How is the curriculum communicated to parents? How much homework is given? How is feedback managed? What provision is there for children who are struggling or need more challenges?

- **Extended services**. Does it offer breakfast or homework clubs? Is there a system of feeder schools or a nursery for younger siblings?

- **PTA**. Is there an active parent and teacher association? How involved are parents in the school?

- **Ofsted report**. How was the school rated in the most recent inspection? What areas were marked for improvement and what is the school doing to address this?

- **Discipline**. How is discipline managed? What is the school's anti-bullying policy? How is the playground supervised?

❀ HOW TO CHOOSE A SECONDARY ❀ SCHOOL

- **What your child wants**. Unlike primary school, your child may have very definite ideas about which secondary school they wish to go, often heavily influenced by their peer group. Listen and discuss your child's concerns, although bear in mind that 11-year-olds make friends easily. Choose the school you feel is best, over the most popular choice with your child's friends.

- **League tables**. Treat with caution. They are notoriously difficult to read accurately and give little indication of the actual experience of attending that school or its intake. Ofsted reports present a more rounded view of the quality of teaching and the school's socio-economic profile. Check how many children are achieving A*–C scores in English and maths, as well as achieving five GCSEs in strong subjects such as science, maths, languages and English; these are minimum requirements, yet not all schools even offer the capacity to study languages or all science subjects.

- **Choice**. Many secondary schools in England have the option to specialise in a particular area. If this applies to your school, are pupils obliged to choose this subject at GCSE? What extra-curricular activities are offered? Is there the opportunity to play in an orchestra, join an athletics team, participate in trips abroad?

- **Higher education**. How is higher education supported or promoted? What careers advice is offered? Are there links with particular universities?

❀ FIRST DAY AT SCHOOL ❀

PRIMARY

- Read books about the first day and discuss the types of activities they might do.

- Listen to and acknowledge your child's fears.

- Double-check arrangements for the first day, particularly if entry is being staggered over several weeks. Check what documents are required to register.

- Attend any open days which will introduce your child to their teacher and classroom.

- Encourage independence in your child by ensuring they are able to get dressed and go to the toilet by themselves.

SECONDARY

- Speak positively about the school, even if you have misgivings.

- Practise the route to school, particularly if your child is going by themselves.

- Give them emergency money in case they need to make a phone call or take further transport.

- Check the timetable together and work out what kit is needed on what day. Get your child into the habit of packing their school bag the night before.

- Ensure your child has plenty of time to eat a good breakfast.

- Take time to chat with your child about their day, though try to avoid pestering them with questions immediately after returning from school.

- Encourage friendships by letting your child invite friends back after school or at the weekends.

- Out-of-school activities will encourage a wider circle of friends or over-reliance on one small group. Be careful, however, not to over-schedule your child's week when they are still coming to terms with a new environment.

Does your child need extra tuition?

- *Work with the school first: find out why or if your child is struggling and what the teachers recommend.*
- *Extra coaching is often most effective if geared towards a very specific target, such as an entrance exam.*
- *Ongoing tutoring can help build the confidence of a child struggling in a mainstream environment.*

- *Ask at school: some teachers are prepared to tutor in their spare time.*
- *Take an interest: tutoring works best when parents ask questions, check their child's progress and track what the tutor is doing.*
- *Don't over-schedule: allow your child time to wind down and take a break from learning.*

Pocket tip 🦋

Tutoring should never be a substitute for good effort in class.

❋ HELPING WITH HOMEWORK ❋

Showing interest and giving support with your child's homework will encourage a positive attitude towards learning and school. You will benefit by learning more about your child's strengths and weaknesses and spending quality time together.

How you can help

- Provide a quiet, well-lit space equipped with the necessary stationery and resources; keep the television off but allow music.

- Check the homework diary and use it to update the teacher on what your child has found difficult and what they have done well.

- Look out for school-run talks on the curriculum for parents, which will explain teaching methods and what is expected of each child.

- Encourage independent learning by showing your child how to look up a word or a fact rather than just providing the answer.

- Agree on a routine with your child with a set time for homework on schooldays; build in time for your child to wind down and snack first.

- Be positive and give lots of praise: avoid presenting homework as a chore.

- Don't be tempted to do your child's homework for them: your child won't benefit if the school is unaware of their real progress.

- Many schools offer homework clubs if you feel your child is struggling or home is not a calm atmosphere.

Websites to help you help your child with their homework

- www.topmarks.co.uk
- www.learn.co.uk
- www.maths.com
- www.scholastic.co.uk
- www.happychild.org.uk
- www.underfives.co.uk
- www.channel4learning.com/apps/homeworkhigh
- www.bbc.co.uk/schools/parents/

The Department for Children, Schools and Families recommended guidelines for homework

Primary school children

- Years 1 and 2: 1 hour per week
- Years 3 and 4: 1.5 hours per week
- Years 5 and 6: 30 minutes per day

Secondary school children

- Years 7 and 8: 45–90 minutes per day
- Year 9: 1–2 hours per day
- Years 10 and 11: 1.5–2.5 hours per day.

❁ GETTING YOUR CHILD ❁ INTERESTED IN READING

An appreciation for literature and reading will prepare your child for years of education and the workplace, as well as creating a lifelong love of books.

- Have books and newspapers around the house.

- Let your children handle and access your books.

- Let them see you reading and enjoying books.

- Join and use your local library.

- Buy your child magazines as a treat.

- Make storytime an integral part of a bedtime routine.

- Expose your child to as many different types of literature as possible – comics, newspapers, manuals, dictionaries, novels – to encourage creativity in their own writing.

Books every child should read

1.	The Complete Fairy Tales	Brothers Grimm
2.	The Hobbit	J. R. R. Tolkien
3.	The Lion, the Witch and the Wardrobe	C. S. Lewis
4.	Tom's Midnight Garden	Philippa Pearce
5.	Pippi Longstocking	Astrid Lindgren
6.	Charlie and the Chocolate Factory	Roald Dahl
7.	Ballet Shoes	Noel Streatfeild
8.	The Secret Garden	Frances Hodgson Burnett
9.	Five Children and It	E. Nesbit
10.	The Famous Five series	Enid Blyton
11.	The Borrowers	Mary Norton

❁ HOW TO CHOOSE A UNIVERSITY ❁

Ultimately it remains your child's choice but parents can be instrumental in helping their child to prioritise and see the bigger picture. Try not to let your own feelings dominate: you may have your heart set on a doctor in the family but there is little point in your child selecting a course to which they are not totally committed.

Drawing up a shortlist

- **Course**. Many universities specialise in particular subjects, but look beyond the course title as content and requirements vary greatly. Consider how the course is assessed, whether it is exam-based or coursework: would a particular method suit your child's academic temperament better? Many undergraduates change their mind only after starting their first year: how flexible is the choice of subject matter? How easy would it be to change course?

- **Career**. What career guidance does the university offer? How vocational is the course? Are there opportunities for work placements? Are there effective alumni networks?

- **Geography**. City or town, campus or centre-based, close to home or far-flung climes? Does your child like a very active social life? Do they need to live at home? Would they be lost in a very large city?

- **Entrance requirements**. How likely is your child to fulfil the admissions requirements? How flexible are the admissions procedures? What is the back-up plan if they don't make the grade?

- **Facilities**. Does your child have a particular extra-curricular activity? How is an interest in sport or music or journalism or politics catered for?

- **Accommodation**. What is available and how much does it cost? What happens in the second year and what are the options for living out of halls?

- **Funding**. What fees are expected and how much will your child receive in terms of loans and/or grants? How long is the course and how are placements funded? Will your child be able to supplement their living costs with a part-time job?

Ten mothers in literature

1. *Mrs Ramsay*	*To the Lighthouse, Virginia Woolf*
2. *Marmee*	*Little Women, Louisa May Alcott*
3. *Mrs Weasley*	*Harry Potter, J. K. Rowling*
4. *Ma Joad*	*Grapes of Wrath, John Steinbeck*

5.	*Mrs Bennet*	*Pride and Prejudice, Jane Austen*
6.	*Gertrude*	*Hamlet, William Shakespeare*
7.	*Mrs Reilly*	*A Confederacy of Dunces, John Kennedy Toole*
8.	*Mrs Coulter*	*His Dark Materials, Philip Pullman*
9.	*Mrs Portnoy*	*Portnoy's Complaint, Philip Roth*
10.	*Corinne Dollanganger*	*Flowers in the Attic, V. C. Andrews*

THE LATER YEARS

❀ TEENAGE DATING ❀

Coping with the delicate mix of a teenage child's vulnerability and bravado becomes yet more difficult once they start expressing an interest in the dreaded members of the opposite sex. How you handle this need for both protection and friendship depends on your relationship with your child and their level of maturity and experience.

Do

- Show an interest: in their friends, their activities, their likes and dislikes.

- Keep criticism to yourself: if you don't like your child's friends, telling them will only alienate you.

- Let your child make mistakes: it's part of growing up.

- Discuss peer pressure: how will your child handle pressure to conform? Are they confident enough to make their own choices?

- Be open and honest about dating, relationships and sex; keep talking, share your experiences and make time to listen to theirs.

WHAT YOU NEED TO TELL THEM

The typical teenager does not want to hear dating tips from their mother. However, the following list provides some useful points for discussion and may help highlight potential problems.

- **Stick to your own age**. Dating much older people can result in additional pressures, such as getting physical too soon.

- **Go out with lots of people**. The teenage years are not the time to settle down. Keep it fun and light-hearted.

- **Focus on your friends**. Boyfriends and girlfriends come and go but friends will last a lifetime, so don't ditch them for your current squeeze.

- **Date in groups**. There is safety in numbers and hanging out in groups is often more fun and less pressurised.

- **Set limits**. Think and decide before a date where the boundaries are and don't let anyone change your mind.

- **Have a plan**. Make arrangements for a first date in advance and don't feel forced to do something against your instincts.

'PROM' NIGHT

The school dance, or prom, is becoming an increasingly common rite of passage for UK school leavers, although thankfully it is still just a special night to mark the end of the school years, rather than a US-style alcohol-fuelled extravaganza. Here's how to help keep it that way:

- Keep the expense down: agree an overall budget for the night and then leave it up to your child as to how they spend it, eg they may opt for a cheaper outfit but have their hair professionally styled.

- Part of the fun is getting ready: a daughter may like to host a pre-prom party for her and her friends to get ready. Supply drinks and nibbles and plenty of hairspray.

- Shopping for a dress or suit together is a great opportunity for some quality mother–daughter/son time.

- Discuss beforehand access to alcohol and the need for personal safety. Ensure that your child and their friends recognise the importance of sticking together and looking after each other.

- Get an itinerary for the night: if they're going to be driven, find out by whom and lay down some non-negotiable rules about drinking and driving.

- Make sure you can be contacted at all times on the night and agree a code word which your child can use to communicate that they are in an uncomfortable situation.

- Check with the other parents if your child tells you a plan is okay, 'Because everyone else is going to.'

❀ LEARNING TO DRIVE ❀

Even the best of buddies parent–child relationship can be strained to the limit by the fraught demands of teaching a teenager to drive. Unless you have near-saintly levels of patience and an old banger you really don't care about, it is best to call in the professionals to teach the basics at least.

Pocket tip 🦋

The best role model is yourself: drive safely, observe the Highway Code and your child will imitate you.

- Book a professional driving school to teach your child and save your driving expertise for back-up practice.

- For a first practice together, choose an early Sunday morning with clear dry weather. A vacant car park is an ideal place to start.

- Focus on the driving and avoid using the one-to-one time to raise other issues.

- Aim to be supportive and encouraging with plenty of praise; hold back on the criticism. Avoid shouting, swearing or loud gasps of fear.

❀ PREPARING FOR UNIVERSITY ❀

Sending your child off into the great unknown can turn the most confident parent into a whole heap of worry. Help smooth those difficult first few weeks by making sure that your child at least has the basics to hand.

Essentials checklist

- Passport photos
- Room insurance
- Passport or driving licence
- NHS number
- National Insurance number
- TV licence if applicable
- Discount travel pass
- Bank account details
- Address book and email/phone contacts
- Local map
- Doctor and dentist details

What your child should know

- A few simple recipes.
- How to use a washing machine.
- The basics of budgeting.
- How to plan their own time: studying, social life, activities.

❀ HOW TO HANDLE EMPTY NEST ❀ SYNDROME

Many women are surprised at the strength of their emotions once children begin to leave home. Feelings of loss and redundancy can be a form of grieving, particularly if the departure coincides with other major life changes, such as the menopause or retirement.

If your main focus has been caring for your children over many years, learning how to fill the void left by their absence can be a long but not always negative process. It might also be the first time in years that your partner and yourself are living together alone: consider it as the perfect opportunity to recharge your relationship and focus on the future.

Practical steps

- Ration calls to your son or daughter: two a week is probably enough.

- Contact by email or text is less intrusive.

- Create plans for the weeks following their departure to keep yourself busy.

- Make physical exercise part of your new daily routine.

- Stretch your mind with a new hobby or adult education course.

- Look afresh at your home and consider renovations or decorating.

- Write a list of places you've always wanted to see, home and abroad, and start ticking them off.

- Take up volunteer work to expand your contacts.

- Meet and chat with friends who have been through the same experience.

It kills you to see them grow up. But I guess it would kill you quicker
if they didn't.
Barbara Kingsolver

❀ HOW TO ORGANISE A WEDDING ❀

GETTING INVOLVED

There is something peculiar about the prospect of seeing your child getting married that can turn even the most rational mother loopy. The demands of bringing two families together and organising the reception can be extremely taxing, even without the emotional intricacies of seeing your child getting wed. If there are additional complexities to consider, such as divorced parents or step-families, it is not surprising that organising a wedding can be more a source of stress than joy.

Nowadays there is no set role for any member of the wedding party, beyond the legal technicalities of getting married. Therefore, the mother's role is to do exactly what the couple asks of her. This might be all or nothing, depending on your relationship with them, their age and situation.

Pocket fact

Many children still rely heavily on their mothers for help and guidance in planning their big day.

Whatever the style of wedding, recognise that the couple's choices might not be the same as yours. Rituals and fashions surrounding the ceremony have changed and there are no set rules. Appreciate the differences and be supportive. A bride-to-be in particular may be feeling tense and fraught in the run-up to the big day and you will probably bear the brunt of her anxiety. The newlyweds will appreciate your support and understanding in the long run.

MOTHER OF THE BRIDE'S TRADITIONAL ROLE

Before the day, help the bride

- Order the wedding stationery.
- Choose the flowers.
- Draw up the guest list.
- Write the invites and coordinate the RSVPs.
- Plan the reception (venue, catering, music) and seating plan.
- Select a wedding dress.

On the day

- Check that the flowers, the cars and the photographer have all turned up and are correct.

- Oversee the dressing of the bridesmaids and help the bride with her dress.

- Travel to the church with the bridesmaids. The mother of the bride is the last to be seated.

- After the ceremony the bride and the groom's parents, the bridesmaids, best man and ushers witness the signing of the registry.

- The bride's mother leaves the venue with the groom's father, walking behind the best man and chief bridesmaid.

- The parents of the bride are the first persons to greet the arriving guests in the reception, with the mother of the bride first in line.

- The mother of the bride is seated to the left of the groom on the top table with the bride's new father-in-law on her left.

- After the first dance of the newlyweds, the mother of the bride dances with the groom's father and the bride's father dances with the groom's mother.

MOTHER OF THE GROOM'S TRADITIONAL ROLE

Before the wedding

- Introduce your family to that of the bride.

- Arrange your side of the guest list, including chasing up RSVPs and organising accommodation for guests.

- Liaise with the couple and the bride's family to clarify who will pay for what.

- Check with the bride to see if there is anything specific you can help with, such as researching flowers or finding a cake supplier.

- Host the rehearsal supper, if there is one.

On the day

- The groom's mother leaves the venue with the bride's father, walking behind the best man and chief bridesmaid.

- The mother of the groom is seated to the right of the father of the bride on the top table with the bride on his left.

- Smile. A lot.

PRACTICAL TIPS FOR THE MOTHER OF EITHER THE BRIDE OR THE GROOM

- Clarify exactly what you are prepared to pay for (music, catering, flowers, bar, favours, bridesmaids' outfits and so on), and what happens if the plans run over budget.

- If the couple prefer to cover expenses themselves, offer to pay for something distinct as a gift, such as the cake or flowers.

- Remember that even if you are footing the whole bill, the style of the event is the couple's choice.

- Contact the bride/groom's family if you don't already know them and arrange to meet for an informal dinner.

- The guest list is a typical source of contention: draw up your list of invitees early and suggest to the bride/groom's mother to do likewise. Meet to discuss and see where compromises can be made, but remember that the final decision lies with the couple.

- If you think the bride's choice of dress is unflattering, be tactful: suggest looking at a range of styles.

- Play to your strengths: perhaps you have calligraphy skills and could write the invites? Or are you renowned for your baking and could make the cake?

What to wear

- It is polite to check with the bride whether she has any specific wishes—for example, what colour the bridesmaids are wearing, avoiding white, cream or black.
- Use a personal shopper: many large department stores offer this service for free.
- Compare notes with the mother of the bride or groom to avoid clashes.
- Don't shop alone: take a trusted friend whose style you admire to give you an honest opinion.
- Think of your usual style and buy the nicest, classiest version of this in a luxury fabric such as silk. For example, if you usually wear trousers, invest in a fantastic trouser-suit.

❀ BEING A GOOD MOTHER-IN-LAW ❀

Just when you thought that being a mother was complicated enough, you acquire in-laws. The unfortunate subject of many puns and jokes, the over-bearing and insensitive mother-in-law has long been a figure of fun and dislike.

But there is no reason why the relationship between a mother and her child's partner should always be fraught; indeed, understanding and respecting each other's abilities as mothers and wives can lead to a mutual source of support and understanding.

Pocket tip 🦋
Nurturing a good relationship with your son- or daughter-in-law can only improve the bond with your own child.

Establishing a good relationship with your son- or daughter-in-law

- Always call first before dropping in.

- Be flexible: they may have other family commitments and can't necessarily see you every Christmas.

- Ask before helping or giving advice, particularly regarding childcare or domestic duties.

- Treat all your children and grandchildren equally.

- Aim for mutual respect, not a mother–child relationship: your son/daughter-in-law already has a mother.

- Get to know them: spend time together, take them out for lunch.

- If you have a daughter-in-law in particular, try not to think that she should do everything the way you do. Look for the positive and avoid criticism.

- Give gifts unconditionally: if you are helping your child and their partner out with money, give it freely without conditions attached.

- If your in-laws' flaws don't bother your child, it would be helpful if you didn't point them out.

- Never interfere in your child's marriage.

❂ BECOMING A GRANDMOTHER ❂

Never have children, only grandchildren.
Gore Vidal

Being a grandmother is the reward for years of hard child-rearing: plenty of love and fun without the responsibility and resentment. The traditional granny character of grey hair and walking stick is increasingly out of date now that many grandparents are still working and have a full and active life of their own. Fitting in time to see the grandchildren is often the main challenge, particularly now that many families are geographically distant. However, in an age when divorce is common, grandparents can play a crucial role in providing a source of stability and consistency, a welcome counterpoint to tensions between parent and child.

Pocket tip 🦋
Avoid the temptation to offer advice and instead give freely what parents are usually short of: time and patience.

If your baby is 'beautiful and perfect, never cries or fusses, sleeps on schedule and burps on demand, an angel all the time,' you're the grandma.
Teresa Bloomingdale

Do

- Keep in touch: no matter how busy your life is, phone frequently, write and visit.

- Make your house safe: when the grandchildren come to play, move ornaments, shut dogs away, fence off ponds.

- Help your children: give them a lie-in, offer to babysit, cook a meal.

- Equip yourself: keep a few treats in store, get some toys.

- Never contradict or overrule the parents.

- Keep your opinions to yourself on sensitive areas such as weaning, potty-training, discipline.

Pocket fact 🌱

Grandparents provide some care to 82% of children in the UK.

If you live far away
- Send parcels and postcards
- Master email and text, even webcam
- Have the grandchildren to stay by themselves when they are old enough.

The reason grandchildren and grandparents get along so well is that they have a common enemy.
Sam Levenson

Ten things to do with your grandchildren

1. *Look through old photo albums*
2. *Draw a simple family tree using photos*
3. *Make paper chains and paper dolls*
4. *Teach your grandchild how to French knit using loo rolls*
5. *Sit on top of a bus and take a circular route*
6. *Tidy your jewellery box together*
7. *Pay each child 50p to learn a poem by heart*
8. *Make a big tray of old-fashioned fudge*
9. *Let your grandchild teach you their favourite computer game*
10. *Measure their height against a door frame*

LOOKING AFTER YOUR CHILDREN: HEALTH AND SAFETY

❀ BASIC FIRST AID ❀

Keeping your child safe is the most basic requirement of being a mother. From awareness of how to handle everyday cuts and scrapes to familiarity with life-saving techniques, first aid knowledge will give you the confidence that you are creating a safe environment in which your child can explore and grow.

Pocket fact 🌱

Injury is the leading cause of death among children and adolescents aged 0–19 years in England.

Essential family first aid kit

- Adhesive plasters
- Adhesive cloth tape
- Sterile compress dressings
- Sterile gauze pads
- Triangular bandages
- Antiseptic wipes
- Antiseptic ointment
- Aspirin
- Baby paracetamol suspension
- Baby ibuprofen suspension
- Hydrocortisone ointment
- Disposable non-latex gloves
- Scissors

- Tweezers
- Safety pins
- Oral thermometer
- List of emergency contact numbers

RESUSCITATION: ESSENTIAL TECHNIQUES

- Ask someone to call an ambulance.
- If you are by yourself, resuscitate for one minute before calling an ambulance.
- Use adult resuscitation procedures for children over eight.

When dealing with a casualty, always use the following checklist:

1. **A**irway
2. **B**reathing
3. **C**irculation

Child (one to eight years old)

Rescue breath

1. Tilt the head back using one hand on the child's forehead and two fingers under the chin.

2. Pinch the child's nose, closing the nostrils.

3. Place your lips over the child's mouth, creating an airtight seal.

4. Blow gently into the mouth until the chest rises.

5. If the chest rises, the rescue breath is effective.

Cardiopulmonary resuscitation (CPR)

1. Kneel beside the child.

2. Place the heel of your hand on the lower breastbone, in the centre of the chest.

3. Lean vertically over the child, keeping your arms straight. Depress the chest by one-third of its depth. Release the pressure without removing the hand.

4. Repeat 30 times (at a rate of 100 per minute) before giving two rescue breaths.

Baby (under one year)

- Ask someone to call an ambulance.

- If you are by yourself, resuscitate for one minute before calling an ambulance, taking the infant with you.

Rescue breath

1. Check the airway is clear.

2. Cover and seal the baby's mouth and nose using your mouth.

3. Fill your cheeks with air and use this amount.

4. Check to see whether the chest is rising.

CPR

1. Place the baby on a firm surface.

2. Place two fingers in the centre of the chest. It is not necessary to remove clothing.

3. Press down to a third of the chest's depth.

4. Repeat 30 times before giving two rescue breaths.

5. Continue with resuscitation until help arrives.

STINGS AND BITES

Wasp and bee stings

1. If you can see the sting, scrape it sideways with your fingernail or a blunt object.

2. Don't use tweezers.

3. Raise the affected area and apply a cold compress.

4. Neutralise the venom using a mild solution of vinegar or lemon juice. Calamine lotion and/or antihistamine creams will soothe itching.

5. If pain and/or swelling persist, consult a doctor.

Pocket tip 🦋

To treat stings to the mouth and throat, give the casualty an ice cube to suck or a glass of cold water to sip. If swelling develops, dial 999 for an ambulance immediately.

Animal bites

1. Wash the bite wound using soap and warm water.

2. Pat dry using sterile gauze and cover with an adhesive dressing.

3. If the would is deep, control any bleeding by raising the injured part and applying direct pressure. Cover with a sterile dressing and seek medical attention immediately.

SPLINTERS

1. Wash hands thoroughly before removing the splinter.

2. Squeeze the splinter from both sides and below to try and force it out the way it came.

3. If this fails, clean the area, a needle, and a pair of tweezers with iodine solution.

4. Using the needle, scrape the skin above the splinter to open it up. Clasp the splinter with the tweezers and remove it.

5. Wash the area again with warm water and soap and/or iodine solution.

6. Organic material such as wood or thorns is more likely to get infected or cause a reaction. Most splinters will work their own way out of the skin if they can be left alone. Consult your doctor if the splinter is underneath a fingernail.

SCRAPES AND CUTS

1. Run cool water over the area to clean the wound and reduce any swelling. Ice will help numb the pain.

2. Stop any bleeding by applying firm, even pressure with a cloth or sterile gauze.

3. Remain calm and in control even if you don't feel it: your child will pick up on your anxiety.

4. Use a plaster to keep the wound clean. Bright colourful plasters are fun and will distract your child.

5. Check the area for further redness, swelling, discharge or increased pain, which may indicate infection.

6. Ensure that your children's tetanus injections are up to date.

BURNS AND SCALDS

Pocket fact

Every day one child under five in the UK is admitted to hospital with scalds caused by bath water.

Do

- Apply a cool running liquid for at least 10 minutes. If water is not available, other liquids such as milk or juice may be used.
- Carefully remove any jewellery or clothing unless it is sticking to the burn.
- Cover the injury with a sterile dressing to protect from infection. Use a clean plastic bag to cover a hand or foot.
- Always take a child or baby with burns to hospital.

Don't

- Apply very cold water or ice: lowering the body temperature of babies in particular can be dangerous.
- Burst any blisters.
- Apply ointment or anything oily to the affected area.

CHOKING

Child

Check the mouth for the obstruction but avoid a finger sweep. If the child is making a noise, encourage them to cough it out.

If they can't speak, cough or breathe, or are losing consciousness, apply the following procedures in this order:

1. **Five back slaps**. Five slaps on the back between the shoulders blades using the heel of your hand.

2. **Five chest thrusts**. Standing behind the child, clench your fist and pull sharply upwards into the chest every three seconds, up to five times.

3. **Five abdominal thrusts**. Standing behind the child, place your fist between the child's navel and the bottom of the breastbone. Pull upwards, repeating up to five times.

4. Repeat the entire procedure three times before calling an ambulance.

Baby

Look for a flushed face and difficulty in breathing.

1. **Five back slaps**. Lie the baby face down along your forearm, keeping the head low and supporting the body. Slap between the shoulder blades up to five times. Check inside the mouth and continue with chest thrusts if necessary.

2. **Five chest thrusts**. With the baby facing up along your forearm, place two fingers on the lower part of the breastbone. Give up to five sharp thrusts inwards and upwards every three seconds.

3. Repeat the back and chest thrusts sequence up to three times.

If the child or baby falls unconscious, give rescue breaths and chest compressions.

POISONING

- Ask the casualty what has been swallowed.
- Dial 999; give as much information as possible about the poison.
- Don't induce vomiting.

- If the casualty is unconscious, check the airway is clear and apply CPR if necessary.

- If the patient's lips are burnt by the poison, give frequent sips of cold water or milk.

❀ DEALING WITH COMMON ❀ COMPLAINTS

Pocket fact 🌱
The average child catches between six and 10 colds a year.

Colds
- **Symptoms**. Runny or blocked nose, sore throat, headache, mild fever, cough.

- **Treatment**. Antibiotics are ineffective against this very common virus, which usually lasts a week. Ibuprofen or paracetamol will provide relief for aches, shivers and sore throats. Decongestants, in the form of a vapour rub or as an oil that can be added to a pillow or tissue, can help clear a blocked nose.

Conjunctivitis
- **Symptoms**. Redness or inflammation in one or both eyes; discharge or itchy eyes.

- **Treatment**. Warm or cold compresses will ease the discomfort, as can bathing the area in warm boiled water to remove any crust. If it does not clear up in a week, it may be a bacterial infection, in which case your GP can prescribe antibiotic ointment or drops.

Croup
- **Symptoms**. A distinctive barking cough that comes on very suddenly, usually at night, and is often accompanied by noisy breathing, fever and a cold. Children grow out of it by about the age of five.

- **Treatment**. Croup can be frightening for both parent and child, so reassure your child and remain calm yourself. Sit your child up and give water to sip. Steam may help: sit your child on your lap in the bathroom with a hot shower running. If your child has severe difficulty breathing or is blue around the mouth, seek urgent medical attention.

Earache

- **Symptoms**. Redness in the ear, leaking yellowish fluid, pulling and tugging at the ear, a distressed child who can't be comforted. Often occurs three to four days after a cold begins.
- **Treatment**. Pain and fever can be treated with paracetamol suspension. Apply heat using a hot water bottle wrapped in a blanket or a warm moist flannel to soothe the discomfort.

Headlice

- **Symptoms**. Itchy scalp, small white eggs (the 'nits'), grey-brown lice, up to 2mm in size, usually found under the fringe, at the nape of the neck and behind the ears.
- **Treatment**. 'Wet' the hair with plenty of conditioner and comb through using a special headlice comb to remove live lice and eggs. Apply anti-headlice treatment. Repeat the wet combing every three to four days until no lice or eggs or found and repeat anti-headlice treatment in seven days to avoid re-infestation.

Nosebleed

- **Treatment**. Reassure your child and get him or her to sit down (don't let them lie down as this will increase the blood flow and may also result in vomiting). Pinch the soft part of the nose for 10 minutes.

Stomach upset

- **Symptoms**. Vomiting, diarrhoea, stomach pains.
- **Treatment**. Avoid dehydration by giving plenty of fluids. Introduce normal food gradually: bananas, apples, cooked rice, and boiled chicken are ideal. Dairy foods can prolong

diarrhoea so should be eliminated. If your child is showing signs of dehydration such as a dry mouth, decreased urination (six dry nappies in a day) and lack of tears, contact your doctor immediately.

Threadworms

- **Symptoms**. Itchy bottom at night, weight loss and insomnia in severe cases.

- **Treatment**. Over-the-counter medication will kill the worms in a few days. The whole family needs to be treated and hygiene measures should be followed for at least two weeks to avoid re-infestation: frequent handwashing, daily hot-wash of bedding, underwear, and pyjamas, washing the child's bottom every morning, vacuuming mattresses.

Throat infection

- **Symptoms**. Throat pain, difficulty swallowing, fever.

- **Treatment**. Paracetamol and ibuprofen will relieve the pain and fever. Give honey and lemon in hot water to soothe an irritated throat. Bacteria infections respond to antibiotics.

Pocket tip 🦋

To get rid of a wart or verruca, cover the infection with a small circle of duct tape; the wart will drop off in three to four days.

When to keep a child at home

Specific guidelines vary from school to school but generally your child needs to stay at home if they have:

- Fever higher than 38°C (100.4°)
- Vomiting
- Diarrhoea
- Infectious conjunctivitis

Meningitis

Meningitis is the inflammation of the lining around the brain and the spinal cord: there are around 2,000 cases in the UK and the Republic of Ireland every year. It can be very dangerous, so fast action is absolutely essential.

Symptoms

- *High temperature*
- *Very sleepy or too sleepy to wake up*
- *Vomiting and/or refusal to feed*
- *Irritability*
- *Pale, blotchy skin*
- *Cold hands and feet*
- *A stiff body with jerky movements or floppiness*
- *A tense or bulging soft spot (fontanelle) on the top of the head*

Tumbler test: *A septicaemic rash will not fade when a glass tumbler is pressed firmly against it. The rash will be clearly visible through the glass. If this occurs, call for medical advice straightaway. Check paler areas first as the rash is less visible on darker skin.*

❀ MAKING YOUR HOME A SAFE HAVEN ❀

A totally 'child-proof' environment does not exist and arguably nor should it: minor accidents are an essential part of how children learn to negotiate their world. No toddler can learn to walk without first falling over many times. However, creating a safe environment will give you peace of mind and enable your child to play and explore without serious risk.

Pocket fact 🌱

According to the Royal Society for the Prevention of Accidents, over a million children in the UK attend casualty departments each year as a result of accidents in the home.

Parental supervision is clearly the best method of accident prevention but it is all too easy to get distracted by a phone call or the demands of another child. Once your child is on the move, put basic precautions in place to limit the area and materials they can access.

Basic checklist

- Safety gates for stairs, bedrooms and kitchens
- Window locks
- Finger-guards for doors
- Fireguards
- Lockable medicine cupboards
- Filling in or fencing off ponds
- Warning labels and child resistant caps on household chemicals
- Lockable cupboards for all DIY and garden substances
- Smoke alarms

Home safety tips

- Keep stairs free of clutter.

- Secure tall furniture and televisions to the walls so they can't be pulled over.

- Don't leave things beneath a window that can be climbed on.

- Fill in or fence off ponds if you have children under six.

- Plan an escape route in the event of fire and make sure your family is familiar with it.

- Set the domestic hot water system to 46°C or fit a thermostatic mixing valve to taps.

- Always turn the cold water on first when running a bath; test the water temperature with your elbow before letting a child get in.

- Never leave children or babies unsupervised in the bath, even for a moment: if the doorbell rings, take the baby with you.

- Make glass furniture safer by applying shatter-resistant film.

Pocket fact 🌱

According to the Office for National Statistics, 46% of all fatal accidents with children involve house fires.

HOUSEHOLD POISONS

All kinds of household substances can be dangerous if ingested: cosmetics, cleaning agents, laundry products, gardening supplies and so on. Never underestimate what a small child is prepared to put into their mouth, irrespective of its taste or smell. Be particularly cautious with medicines and vitamin products, which are often brightly coloured and designed to be swallowed easily. Keep all products out of a child's reach and ensure that the most hazardous products are locked securely away.

Common poisons found in the home

- Medicines
- Antifreeze
- Windshield washer solutions
- Weed killer
- Drain cleaners
- Toilet bowl cleaners
- Insecticides
- Artificial nail removers

See p 143 for what to do if your child ingests poison.

How to . . . fit a car seat

It is essential to follow the manufacturer's instructions correctly; if you have lost them, contact the manufacturer for a copy.

1. Thread the seatbelt through the appropriate guide on the seat. If the belt is too short, some seats have an alternative route; this will be detailed in the instructions.

2. Push your full weight into the seat as you tighten the belt, which should contain no slack.

3. Make sure that the buckle is clear of the edge of the car seat: it should not be holding the seat in place.

4. To test if the seat is fitted correctly, fasten the harness buckle and grasp the straps. Give it two sharp tugs towards the front of the car. If there is no movement, the seat is installed correctly.

5. Sit your child in the seat: tighten the harness, checking that you can slide two fingers between the harness and your child.

Pocket fact 🌱

In a 30 mph crash an unrestrained child would be thrown forward with a force 30 to 60 times their body weight.

It is safer to sit all children, including babies, in the rear of the car. Never put a rear-facing seat in the front of the car without disabling the airbag, which would strike the seat with considerable force. If you fit a forward-facing seat in the front of the car, ensure that the car seat is as far back as possible to maximise the distance between the child and the airbag.

KEEPING CHILDREN SAFE ONLINE

The internet not only provides an incredible resource for learning and exploration but also presents a real danger in terms of to whom or what your child can be exposed. With technology changing day by day, parents often struggle to keep up-to-date with its challenges. Educate your child from a very young age as to what constitutes safe internet usage. Also, be aware in particular that your child may access the internet from a friend's house or a mobile, therefore bypassing any filters or security strategy in place at home.

What you can do

- Keep the computer in a family or shared room where you can see the monitor.

- Use a family-friendly internet service provider.

- Familiarise yourself with how chatrooms work and the abbreviations that are used.

- Check that the chatrooms your child uses are moderated; show interest in your child's online friends.

- Install safety software or a 'net nanny', including a filter, spyware, and anti-virus programs; use a family friendly search engine, although be aware that they are not always 100% reliable.

- Limit the amount of unsupervised internet time your child is allowed.

- Check the history folder in the browser – which will show all the sites that have been visited; delete and/or block any which are unsuitable.

- If your child has visited somewhere forbidden or given out personal information, try not to be too angry as your child may then lie if they do it again.

What your child needs to know about surfing the internet

- *Never give your name, address, school details or phone number over the internet.*
- *Never send a photo or bank details.*
- *Never enter a chatroom without checking with a parent or guardian first.*
- *Be particularly careful in chatrooms where it is impossible to verify identities.*
- *If someone sends you a nasty or threatening message, don't respond but do tell a parent or guardian.*
- *Don't open attachments unless you know who they are from.*

❁ EMOTIONAL HEALTH ❁

BEREAVEMENT

Like adults, children deal with bereavement in different ways, depending on their personalities and experience. According to their age, children may consider death to be a frightening or confusing concept or as something too abstract to comprehend; they may also be deeply fascinated by the rituals surrounding death. Children of all ages may have limited understanding of their own strong emotions and how to express them, which is where a parent's role can be crucial.

Children often need to find ways to express grief and the accompanying emotions of shock, anger, guilt, confusion and sadness. Don't feel you must suppress your own sadness or tears: if you are able to express your emotions, your children are less likely to bottle up their anxiety.

Younger children will:

- Ask the same questions repeatedly.

- Struggle with abstract concepts, such as 'forever' and 'gone'.

- Vary between deep distress and apparent unconcern.

- Pick up on a parent's upset and sadness.

- Sometimes show distress through changes in behaviour, such as sudden bed-wetting, clinginess, aggression, tantrums, sleep and eating disturbances.

How you can help

- Support and recognise that children grieve, even if they don't do so openly.

- Express your own feelings, showing that it is okay to cry.

- Use plain, factual language, such as 'has died'; phrases such as 'slipped away' can confuse a young child.

- Be prepared to answer many questions, even if that means explaining that you don't have all the answers.

- Offer reassurance and consistency regarding daily routines.

- Involve children in the rituals surrounding death. Children may wish to lay flowers, create a memory box or write a farewell card.

- Prepare a child as to what a funeral involves and give them the choice of whether to attend or not.

- Inform your child's school and ask for their support.

- Keep discussing the person or pet who has died.

DIVORCE

When parents separate, the effects can be potentially traumatic for the whole family. How it is handled can greatly ease the transition into a new family structure. Much more is known nowadays about the emotional ramifications for children, and there is basic guidance available for helping them through the worst.

Children can feel:

- Guilt
- Desire to reunite their parents
- Anxiety over living arrangements
- Grief for the loss of their former family life
- A conflict of loyalty

How you can help

- **Be honest**. Concealing the fact of separation does not protect children and may lead to issues of mistrust.

- **Be appropriate**. Children may not need to be aware of all the details of adult relationships.

- **Be disciplined**. No matter how tempting, resist the urge to criticise your former partner in front of your children.

- **Be fair**. Allow your children to spend time with and love the other parent without feeling they are letting you down.

- **Be reassuring**. Children often blame themselves for marital break-ups. Emphasise that they have done nothing wrong.

- **Be prepared to listen and answer any questions**. Children need to talk and express their feelings to come to terms with the new situation.

- **Be creative**. Children often find it easier to express complex emotions through play rather than speech. Engaging your child in drawing or imaginative activities may help them share difficult feelings.

- **Be consistent**. In uncertain times, both older and younger children can gain security from familiar routines, whether that applies to bedtime habits or weekend activities.

BULLYING

Seeing your child become the target of bullying can bring the most primeval maternal instincts of protection and defence to the fore.

Thankfully, there is now a greater awareness of the profound and negative impact that bullying can have on all aspects of a child's life. Schools in particular are obliged to take it more seriously and a parent concerned that their child is being bullied should enlist their support in taking practical steps.

Possible signs of bullying

Your child is:

- Not wanting to go to school
- Regularly coming home with cuts and bruises
- Becoming silent and withdrawn
- Displaying increased aggression at home
- Performing badly academically
- Showing increased anxiety and signs of insomnia

Contacting the school

- Make an appointment to see your child's class teacher and explain the situation in a non-confrontational manner.

- Check whether your child is being excluded from playground games, or appears unhappy and isolated.

- Ask about the school's anti-bullying policy and how it is implemented: is there a 'Friendship Bench', for example?

- Meet with the head of year or head teacher and check the level of supervision when the incidents are taking place.

- Ask for a follow-up meeting in a month's time to see whether the situation is improving.

Don't

- Go storming in to the school when you are very angry or upset.

- Assume that the school is aware of the problem.

- Ignore what is happening and hope it will go away; bullying is not an inevitable part of growing up and can have serious consequences.

- Keep your child at home: it is regarded as an unauthorised absence and you could be prosecuted. If the situation has deteriorated to the extent that you feel school is no longer safe, contact your local education authority's education welfare officer and ask them to intervene.

Do

- Take time every day to talk with your child. Discuss your own day and ask open-ended questions in order to prompt your child to talk.

- Help your child develop coping strategies: discuss what he or she might do next time they are confronted. Decide on different retorts or actions your child might use.

- Keep a diary of bullying incidents.

- Encourage and widen your child's circle of friends by inviting other children over for playdates.

- Build up your child's confidence by developing out-of-school activities, which will also help them to realise that school is not the be-all and end-all of daily life.

Pocket tip 🦋

Martial arts can be a good option for improving self-protection skills and confidence.

When your child is the bully

It can be even more upsetting for a mother to realise that her child is capable of bullying.

- Tell your child about the accusation and ask them for an explanation.

- Ask the teacher whether there were other children involved and who was the ringleader.

- Ask your child what they think about the victim and how they might feel.

- What would they want done if the bullying was happening to them?

- Ask for supervision to be increased.

- Check whether your child could also be being bullied.

- Request to be kept informed of any further incidents immediately.

SIBLING RIVALRY

The great advantage of living in a large family is that early lesson of life's essential unfairness.
Nancy Mitford

When a new sibling arrives

- Prepare your child for the new arrival: look through some of the many children's books that deal with new babies in the family.

- Make sure that the first time your older child meets the new baby, your arms are empty to give them a big hug.

- Give a big present 'from' the baby to the older child.

- Keep their routine as normal as possible.

- Prioritise the needs of the toddler, even if that means putting down a crying baby to attend the needs of your older child.

- Expect regression: your toddler may reassert their place as the baby and return to bed-wetting, wanting to be fed or speaking in baby-language.

Older children

- Avoid making comparisons, either directly or in conversations that children will overhear.

- Praise children for their unique abilities and don't use labels such as 'the academic one', or 'sporty', or 'difficult'.

- Don't play referee: if no one is getting hurt then take a step back and allow them to work it out between themselves.

- Encourage children to compete primarily with themselves (*Can they run faster than they did yesterday? Can they tidy up better than usual?*) rather than each other.

- Teach respect for personal space and belongings: no one borrows someone else's stuff without permission.

- Listen and acknowledge any resentment (*I understand you are angry; I realise his behaviour is making you cross*) and allow your children to express anger constructively, not through fighting and shouting.

If you've never been hated by your child, you've never been a parent.
Bette Davis

SOME MUCH-NEEDED ME TIME

❁ FINDING TIME FOR YOURSELF ❁

NEW MOTHERHOOD

Motherhood can be the strangest mix of marvel and anxiety. Feelings of love and wonder for your new baby are easily and frequently mixed with a sense of isolation and overbearing responsibility. The dramatic change in role from working in a professional environment to being a stay-at-home mum, often results in conflicting and negative emotions. Building a support network of friends in a similar position can be crucial to avoiding the worst feelings of loneliness and depression.

Where to find support

- **Parenting groups**. The National Childbirth Trust (NCT) and La Leche league host coffee mornings and 'Bumps and Babies' groups for which you don't always have to be a member to join.

- **Health centres and/or SureStart centres**. These run breastfeeding clinics, drop-in play sessions, toy libraries, etc.

- **Local libraries**. Often hold weekly baby storytime sessions.

- **Baby classes**. Baby yoga, baby massage, music classes, baby gym, mother and baby cinema sessions.

- **Playgroups**. Your local library and council will have a list of local sessions. Most are inexpensive and suitable for all young babies.

- **Online communities**. There are many mother- and/or parent-focused websites with chat forums for support and problem-solving, and which offer anonymity.

Ten useful websites for mothers

1. www.mumsnet.com
2. www.parentlineplus.org.uk
3. www.netmums.com
4. www.babycentre.co.uk
5. www.kellymom.com
6. www.badmothersclub.co.uk
7. www.bbc.co.uk/children
8. www.activityvillage.co.uk
9. www.motheratwork.co.uk
10. www.nhsdirect.nhs.uk

POST-NATAL DEPRESSION

About one-third of new mothers will experience depression that is more serious than the very common 'baby blues' that often follow childbirth. It is crucial for your health and that of your family that you seek help from your partner, trusted friends and your health visitor if you feel you are vulnerable to post-natal depression (PND). It can be difficult to diagnose as not every mother will experience the same symptoms. However, if you think you have several of the following signs you should seek help:

- Tiredness
- Excessive anxiety about the baby
- Insomnia
- Lack of self-esteem
- Feelings of inadequacy as a mother
- Lack of interest in one's appearance or health
- Emotionally distant from the baby: a sense that they would be better off without you

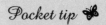

Pocket tip

If you are crying more than your baby, consult your GP.

TAKING CARE OF YOURSELF

Mothers are extremely good at caring for everyone but themselves. While ensuring that everyone else is happy and thriving, it is all too easy to forget about yourself. Years of putting other people first may even result in not knowing who or what we want or how to achieve it. Yet it is crucial that mothers take regular time out, not least because an over-stressed mother facing burnout is of no help to her family.

Do

- Have an evening off: forget the housework, turn off the computer and phone, and take a long bath with a glass of wine.
- Get up half an hour earlier and enjoy a cup of tea in peace.
- Book tickets in advance – sport, theatre, music, cinema, exhibitions.
- Exercise: regular physical activity brings a multitude of mental and physical benefits. Push the buggy around the park. Go late-night swimming. Cycle to work.
- Children swaps: arrange with a friend to care for each other's children once a week.
- Adult education: find an evening class in something you have always been interested in.

FUN IDEAS JUST FOR YOU

Activity	What?	Where?
Exercise	Running, cycling, swimming, yoga, power walking, Pilates, badminton	Leisure centre, private gym
Creative	Knitting, choir, photography, card-making, drawing, creative writing, music appreciation, dress-making	Local craft shops, department store, adult education college
Educational	Book group, DIY, first aid, languages, book-keeping, wine-tasting, carpentry, computing and IT	Local library, local bookshop, adult education or further education (FE) college

How to . . . start a book club

We read to know we are not alone.
C. S. Lewis

- Joining a book club is a good opportunity to share a love of reading and create conversation about something other than childcare. Most libraries and local bookshops now run their own book clubs but if joining a group of strangers seems off-putting, setting up your own is straightforward.

- There is no established structure for a book club but a group of between six and 10 people is a good number to create a discussion, while still allowing everyone a chance to speak. Ask around acquaintances or invite three friends to join and ask them to recruit three more people.

- Meeting once a month usually allows sufficient time to read a book without it becoming burdensome.

- Keep the meetings informal, perhaps in a café or pub; if you prefer the privacy of someone's home, just provide drinks and nibbles to avoid the hosting becoming onerous.

- Draw up a reading-list at the first meeting or take turns to suggest a book but make certain there is general agreement to ensure commitment to reading the book. Consider less obvious choices for a more challenging selection: travel writing, political memoirs, poetry or history.

- Each meeting can be as informal or structured as you wish, though it helps to stimulate discussion if, perhaps, the host introduces the book or provides topics for debate. Agree to keep conversation to the book for at least the first hour.

❁ WORK ❁

The shift to returning to work after becoming a mother is huge, both in practical and emotional terms: your priorities have changed and 24 hours just isn't long enough to deal with them all. It is important to make time during your maternity leave to adjust to this profound shift in your day-to-day life and minimise the impact of any potential problems.

Pocket fact 🌱

In England and Wales, 68% of women with dependent children are employed and 38% work part-time.

Before returning to work

- **Make contact with your employer**. Meet colleagues for lunch, give your boss a ring. The workplace won't seem so daunting if you have kept in touch.

- **Organise childcare well in advance, including a settling-in period**. If finances allow, start your childcare a week before you return to work in order to give yourself time to deal with any niggles.

- **Focus on your priorities**. If you are particularly concerned about getting out of the house on time, do a few practice runs; if you prefer your child to eat homemade food, stock up the freezer.

- **Anticipate emergencies**. Arrange with your partner how you will handle, for example, who covers if your child is ill, if your child minder lets you down, if you are delayed at work, etc.

- **Give yourself a boost**. If budget allows, get a new haircut or buy a pair of shoes – something to help you feel good about walking back into the workplace.

Balancing work and family

- **Mornings**. Do as much as possible the night before, such as packing bags, putting out shoes and coats etc. Teach independence from early on so your children can brush their own hair, get dressed by themselves and so on.

- **Evenings**. Have a routine which includes time to wind down and relax. Prepare food in advance, turn the television off at dinnertime and eat together if possible.

- **Household**. Shop online, not just for food but also for clothes, presents, etc. Save your energy for your family and let the housework go or use the extra income to employ a cleaner or buy prepared food.

- **Childcare**. Keep communication clear: use a contact book whereby your childminder can describe their day and highlight any issues. Build a friendly network of local mothers who can help with emergency back-up and playdates.

- **School**. If you feel that you are missing out on parent–teacher association (PTA) events, ask if there is volunteer work to be done in the evenings (many teachers appreciate help with lesson preparation). Arrange a night out for mothers or week-end events: not all parents work Monday to Friday and are grateful for weekend playdates.

- **When a child is sick**. Agree in advance with your partner how this responsibility will be shared. Work from home or split the day with your partner.

- **Emotions**. Accept that feeling guilty is an inevitable part of motherhood and put the negative emotion to one side mentally. Appreciate the fact that your children are settled and thriving. Enjoy the extra income and the break from domestic duties.

RETURNING TO WORK AFTER AN EXTENDED BREAK

Stepping back into a professional environment following years of focusing on the family can seem like a daunting prospect but need not be an impossible task. Whether you have been out of the workplace for two years or 20, this is a great opportunity to re-think what you would like to do.

Take a detailed and in-depth look at yourself. What skills, abilities, values and experience do you have? Ask a couple of friends and your partner for insights.

- What have I done?
- What am I good at?
- What do I enjoy doing that I am also good at?
- What do I want to avoid?

Consider what skills you have been using that are transferable. What would you need to update before you could fit into your new environment? Perhaps you could take advantage of the career break to consider an entirely new direction and/or re-training.

Pocket tip 🦋

If your experience is not relevant or out of date, rewrite your CV so that it is skills-based rather than in chronological order: this helps play down any gaps in your career as well as presenting you as a fully-rounded person, rather than just a work history.

Skills used in child-rearing

- Communication
- Time management
- Multi-tasking
- Budgeting

What may need updating

- IT skills
- Legal knowledge (particularly in the public sector)

VOLUNTEER WORK

Offering your services for free is a great way to add to your CV, update your skills and meet new people. Schools, churches, and local councils and charities are always looking for extra help, which can range from one-off assistance at a fair, to a responsible committee role, to the occasional couple of hours delivering leaflets. Skills such as fundraising, retail and communication are often easily transferable to a corporate environment. Schools- and parent-focused charities in particular usually offer volunteering opportunities that work around the demands of a young family. It is also a great way to boost your self-esteem if you are feeling unconfident about a return to paid work.

Pocket fact 🌱

Timebank.org.uk is a charity that matches your time and skillset with volunteering opportunities in your area.

How to . . . write a cv

Keep it:

- **Specific**. Tailor your CV to the role you are applying for, even if this means writing various versions.

- **Short**. Two sides of A4 pages is ideal.

- **Relevant**. Cut out all extra-curricular activities, educational details, and ancient job history unless they are relevant to the position being applied for. Avoid general terms in the covering letter.

- **Correct**. Ask a friend to double-check it for spelling mistakes and errors.

- **Neat**. CVs should be typed and printed, and easy to read.

How to . . . network

Networking is the most effective way of finding a job, particularly if you wish to explore a new career. The aim is to find out:

- Advice
- Information
- Useful contacts

- Find people who do what you would like to do: research company websites; ask friends and acquaintances; look up college and school alumni; write a list of everyone you know who could be useful.

- Once your contact has been identified, write a polite but open letter asking for a 15–20 minute meeting and enclosing your CV for background information. Make it very clear that you are not asking for a job.

- Ask for specific advice as to what career options are available, how you can best use your abilities, what qualifications are needed, and whether your CV is relevant.

- Solicit information about the current job market: recruitment, good and bad employers, industry experts.

- Thank the contact and follow-up with an thank you letter specifying what you found useful about the meeting.

❂ RELATIONSHIPS: BEING MORE ❂ THAN JUST A MUM

Never marry a man who hates his mother, because he'll end up hating you.
Jill Bennett

Raising children is hard: exhaustion, conflict and resentment can very quickly become an everyday part of family life. Take steps to work with your partner as a necessary part of securing family harmony and your own personal happiness.

Quick ways to keep your relationship strong

- **Touch**. Hug, stroke, squeeze, hold hands, cuddle, tickle.
- **Communicate**. Chat, discuss, phone, text, laugh, argue, make up.
- **Make time**. Date night, lie-in, eat together, catch up, exercise.
- **Help each other**. Encourage, support, listen, accept, adapt.

Pocket fact 🌱

The average age at first marriage in the UK is 31.8 for men and 29.7 for women. The average age of women in England and Wales at the birth of a first child is 27.5 years.

How to work on your relationship

- **Find a babysitter**. Book a night out at least once a month and consider the expense as part of the housekeeping, rather than a luxury. Even a walk together will give you a break from the children and an opportunity to chat. Try to do things that give you a chance to talk rather than just going to the cinema or theatre.

- **A united front**. Discuss how you approach parenting and aim for consistency on issues such as discipline and routines. Constancy will help engender intimacy and cut down on resentment.

- **Be nice**. Surprise your partner with flowers, a special dinner, or an unasked for cup of tea. Show that you are thinking of them and their happiness.

- **Be polite**. Saying 'please', 'thank you' and 'sorry' demonstrates that you appreciate your partner and helps avoid offence.

KEEPING IT ROMANTIC

It is all too easy for a couple to lose each other under the everyday strains of raising children, work, running the house and so on. Make a date night, once a week if possible, where you prioritise your needs as a couple and not just as parents. If having a babysitter is too expensive or awkward then turn off the television, the phone and do something special together at home: remind yourself what you love about your partner.

Ideas for nights in

- Games night: get out the backgammon, cards or Monopoly. Loser buys dinner.

- Take a bath together and pamper each other with a massage, a manicure and pedicure.

- Have an early night and eat dinner in bed.

- Read to each other: take turns both to choose the book and to read aloud.

- Have a picnic in the back garden: pack finger food and place on a blanket on the grass, lie back and look at the stars.

Nights out

- **See something live**. Go to a gig or the theatre.

- **Outdoor cinema**. Don't forget the rug and a bottle of wine.

- **Get cultured**. Visit a late-night opening of a museum or gallery.

- **Exercise together**. Swim in a late night pool.

- **Go dancing**. Take lessons together for some old-fashioned swing.

> *There is only one happiness in life – to love and to be loved.*
> George Sand

MUM'S DIY

This last chapter shows how a certain level of practical knowledge can help get you out of a sticky and/or expensive situation saving both time and money.

How to . . . change a car tyre

You will need: a spare tyre, a jack, a wheel brace, a flat-bladed screwdriver and a pair of gloves.

1. Put on the gloves and get out the spare tyre and the jack (usually found under the cover in the floor of the boot).

2. Prise off the wheel covers of the tyre to be removed using the flat-bladed screwdriver, cutting through anti-theft nylon ties if necessary.

3. Use the wheel brace to loosen all the nuts by about half a turn.

4. Place the jack in the jacking point that is closest to the affected tyre. Place the spare wheel part-way under the car in case the jack slips. Raise the jack until it is 2.5–5cm off the ground.

5. Remove the wheel's nuts and bolts and take off the tyre. Slide it under the car in place of the spare tyre.

6. Fit the spare tyre, tightening the bolts and nuts until they hold the tyre firmly. Remove the old tyre from under the car, lower and remove the jack.

7. Tighten one nut securely, then complete the one diagonally opposite and continue until they are all fastened securely.

8. Drive to the closest garage, where you can check the pressure of the new tyre and have the nuts tightened to the correct torque setting.

How to . . . mend a puncture

You will need: a puncture repair kit (patch, sandpaper, marker, glue), a bucket of water and a pump.

1. Remove the wheel (from a bike, use the quick release lever or unbolt).

2. Remove the inner tyre and inflate. Check for glass, thorns, and debris. Remove the tyre completely from the rim and check inside and out.

3. Submerge part of the tyre in a bucket of water and look for bubbles escaping. Once you locate the puncture, mark it with chalk or pencil.

4. Let the inner tube dry and then roughen up the area around the puncture hole using the sandpaper. Cover the hole with glue and leave to dry until the glue is tacky. Place the patch centred over the puncture and smooth, removing any air bubbles.

5. Place one edge of the tyre back inside the rim and replace the inner tube, beginning at the valve.

How to . . . put up shelves

You will need: shelving (cut to desired length), brackets, wall plugs, screws, a screwdriver, a pencil, a tape measure, a spirit level, an electric drill and a stud finder/electrical locator.

1. Check the wall for wiring and/or a wall stud if the wall is plasterboard (rather than masonry–brick or stone) by drilling a small hole: if wood shavings appear, you are drilling into timber. Plan to locate the brackets well away from any wiring and preferably on a wall stud.

2. Pencil the desired location of the shelf. Divide the length of the shelf by four and measuring this distance in from each end, mark where each bracket will go. Use the level to check for discrepancies in height and pencil in each screw hole through the bracket.

3. Drill a small hole at each of the screw hole marks. Insert and tap each plug until it is flush with the wall.

4. Once the plugs are fixed, attach the brackets using the screws. They should fit snugly against the wall.

5. After the shelves have been placed on each set of brackets, check for any discrepancies using the spirit level.

Pocket tip 🦋

Pushing down slightly on the shelf may be sufficient to make it perfectly level.

How to . . . hang a picture or mirror

You will need: an electric drill, a hammer, and a few screws and wall plugs.

Determine whether the wall is masonry or cavity/plasterboard.

If the wall is masonry

1. Create a pilot hole using an electric drill.

2. Push in a wall plug, checking that it is securely embedded.

3. Insert the screw.

If the wall is cavity

1. Check the wall for wiring using an electrical locator. Locate a stud either by tapping (the wall will sound hollow between timbers) or using a stud finder.

2. If screwing into plasterboard, use a spiral fixing or a spring toggle to secure the screw. Plasterboard is thin and soft and won't support the weight of heavy objects otherwise.

How to . . . make curtains

1. **Measure**. Measure the window. Double the actual width of the window to gauge the width of the curtains and ensure they hang properly. For height, measure from the curtain rings to below the window sill, or to the desired length.

2. **Fabric**. Mark the fabric using a ruler and tailor's chalk to get as straight a line as possible. Cut the fabric using sharp scissors.

3. **Pattern**. If you are using a fabric with a very large pattern, try to ensure that the main part of the pattern falls just above the bottom hem – this looks more appealing.

4. **Hems**. Fold over half an inch of fabric to make a hem and use a hot iron to press into place; pin to secure. Fold the bottom hem again to create a double hem, which will help the curtains hang better. Mitre the corners first to make them neater and less bulky. (Press the hems, then unfold them out. Fold in the triangle of the corner and pin in place before re-folding and sewing the side and bottom hems.)

5. **Sew**. Using a sewing machine, sew the pressed hem, placing the stitch close to the edge of the hem. Use a couple of backstitches to secure the thread before cutting.

How to . . . bleed a radiator

You will need: the radiator key and a tea towel.

1. Switch off the central heating. If it is a sealed system, plan to reduce the overall pressure of the entire system (consult the manual), and remember to top up the system afterwards from the main cold water feed.

2. Check that the valves at the bottom of the radiator are open.

3. Using the radiator bleed key, insert it onto the brass bleed screw (usually at the top of the radiator).

4. Using the tea towel to shield your hand and catch any drips, slowly turn the screw anti-clockwise about half a turn: there should be a hissing sound.

5. As soon as water squirts out, tighten the screw.

Pocket tip 🦋

Only bleed one radiator a day to avoid losing pressure from the boiler.

How to . . . mend a dripping tap

You will need: a screwdriver, an adjustable spanner, a piece of cloth, wire wool, a replacement washer (usually 1.25cm ($\frac{1}{2}$ inch) for basin and sink taps; 1.8cm ($\frac{3}{4}$ inch) for bath taps).

1. Turn off the water supply using the stopcock (usually found under or near the kitchen sink).

2. Turn on the tap to drain the water and place the plug in the sink to catch anything you may drop.

3. Capstan head tap (traditional): remove the cover to reveal the hexagonal nut. Unscrew the nut to reach the jumper which holds the washer and replace the washer.

4. Shrouded head (modern): remove the central fixing screw holding the head shroud in place, using the screwdriver. The head screw can then be removed to reveal the jumper and washer.

5. Once the washer has been levered off, it should be cleaned using wire wool.

Eco-tip

A dripping tap wastes around two litres of water every hour.

How to . . . oil a squeaking door

You will need: lubricating oil (silicone or graphite, even olive oil will do).

1. Begin with one hinge; move the door back and forwards while applying the oil.

2. Apply a little at first, listening until you hear the squeaking stop.

3. If the squeaking continues, removes the hinges and clean inside and out, removing any rust with wire wool.

4. If there is further squeaking, check and clean the door handle and the screws attaching the hinge. If the door is rubbing against the frame, sand down the area.

How to . . . change a plug and/or a fuse

You will need: a screwdriver, a new plug and a wire-stripper.

1. Unscrew the screw in the underside of the plug and remove the top cover. If there is also a clamp across the wire, loosen the screws holding it in place and the brass screws holding each wire into the pin. Remove the plug and take out the fuse.

2. If the bare flex at the tip of each wire is in good condition, connect the wires to the terminals of the new plug. Wiring is coloured: blue for neutral, brown for live and green and yellow for earth. Modern plugs are clearly marked for E (earth), L (live) and N (neutral). Ensure the colour of each wire connected to the terminal is correct and secure the flexes using a small screwdriver.

3. If the wires are damaged, trim the cord and sheathing to make new wire connections. Cut to the required length and remove 12mm of insulation from the end of each wire using wire strippers.

4. Insert the cord into the new plug so that the sheathed flex is tightly gripped by either the clamp and screws, or the plastic grip. Check the fuse is the appropriate size for the appliance.

5. Replace the plug cover and check that the appliance works.

Pocket fact 🌱

Suggested ratings for fuses: for appliances up to 720W: 3amp; for appliances from 720W to 3kW: 13amp.

How to . . . fit a smoke alarm

1. Position a smoke alarm as close to the centre of a room as possible and at least 30cm away from the nearest wall.

2. Don't place smoke alarms in the kitchen, bathroom or garage as cooking fumes, steam and exhaust fumes will set them off all the time.

3. If your home is multi-storey, fit an alarm on each level.

4. Check the alarm weekly and replace the battery once a year. Every six months vacuum through the casing to remove dust.

How to . . . paint a room

1. Wipe down walls and woodwork with a sponge, hot water and a splash of household cleaner.

2. Fill in any holes using Polyfilla.

3. Sand down any gloss-painted or varnished surfaces, or remove the paint using a paint stripper.

4. Pour a small quantity of paint into a paint kettle. Start with a primer and undercoat on the woodwork, followed by two coats of emulsion on the walls, and finish with a top coat around the woodwork.

Pocket tip 🦋

One-coat gloss paints are available, but applying two coats gives a better, more professional finish.

5. If using a roller, dampen it first with water or the appropriate thinner. Squeeze out excess moisture onto a piece of paper (not newspaper).

6. Fill the roller tray half full with the paint, and place the roller into the middle of the tray, rolling it back and forth.

7. Repeat a couple of times until the paint has worked into the roller. Take care not to overload it with paint, as it will drip and slide across the surface.

8. Paint a 2sq m area at a time. Roll the paint on in a zigzag pattern without lifting the roller from the wall, painting a

large M or W shape. Fill in the wall with more horizontal or vertical zigzag rolling. Raise the roller slowly only when finished so it does not leave a mark.

9. Move onto another unpainted area, and repeat the zigzag technique, ending it just below or next to the first painted patch. Smooth the new application, and blend it into the previously finished area.

10. To paint up to a line where two edges or colours meet, use a brush with bevelled bristles. Paint several strokes perpendicular to the edge. Smooth over these strokes with one long stroke, painting the edge next to the corner first. Where the wall meets the ceiling, use short downward strokes on the wall first and then smooth horizontal strokes.

11. To paint a ceiling, make strokes toward the centre of the room, away from the wall.

12. Finally, paint a smooth horizontal stroke that follows the direction of the wall. Even when using the same colour on adjoining surfaces, use this method to prevent unsightly drips and runs.

Pocket tip 🦋

Store brushes overnight in a covered tin, or wrapped in clingfilm.

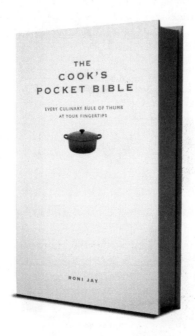